GUNTER SWOBODA AND LORIN JOSEPHSON

Making Good Men Great: Surfing the New Wave Of Masculinity

Special Edition

First published by Bonfire Realities, A Bonfire Cinema imprint

2025

Copyright © 2025 by Gunter Swoboda and Lorin Josephson

All rights reserved. No part of this publication may be reproduced, stored or transmitted in any form or by any means, electronic, mechanical, photocopying, recording, scanning, or otherwise without written permission from the publisher. It is illegal to copy this book, post it to a website, or distribute it by any other means without permission.

Gunter Swoboda and Lorin Josephson asserts the moral right to be identified as the author of this work.

Gunter Swoboda and Lorin Josephson has no responsibility for the persistence or accuracy of URLs for external or third-party Internet Websites referred to in this publication and does not guarantee that any content on such Websites is, or will remain, accurate or appropriate.

First edition

ISBN: 9780999266823

Cover art by Jemi Koo
Editing by Molly Schinn
Editing by Diamond Perkins
Proofreading by Corey Lee
Proofreading by Emilia Osborne

This book was professionally typeset on Reedsy.
Find out more at reedsy.com

Dedication

This book is dedicated to the woman who taught me to respect women, my mother.

Rita Malvine Swoboda
1932-2016

and to my co-author, partner and wife

Lorin Josephson, RN, BA (Hons.), MA

Contents

Foreword		ii
Acknowledgments		iv
Introduction		1
1	Traditional Masculinity	11
2	I want to raise the bar. I want Good Men to become Great!	22
3	So, how did we get into this mess?	29
4	The Iron Age Warrior in the Digital Age	37
5	Patriarchy: The Four Toxic Values	42
6	The Psychological Consequences of Patriarchal Values: -...	62
7	The Issue of Good & Great	124
8	The Next Phase of Our Evolution	143
9	Men and Relationships	152
10	Humans are Relational	160
11	Modern Masculinity	168
12	Being a Great Dad	183
13	Men Within Society	198
Glossary of Terms		210
References		217
About the Author		222

Foreword

In the vast sea of literature addressing masculinity, *Making Good Men Great: Surfing a New Masculinity* emerges as a beacon of insight and guidance. In a world where traditional notions of manhood are being challenged and redefined, this book is not just timely but essential.

Swoboda and Josephson navigate the tumultuous waters of contemporary masculinity with a deft hand, blending scholarly rigour with practical wisdom. Drawing from their extensive experience and research, they offer a compelling framework for understanding and cultivating a new kind of masculinity—one rooted in authenticity, empathy, and accountability.

"Making Good Men Great" is not merely a theoretical treatise; it's a blueprint for personal growth and societal transformation. With clarity and compassion, the authors invite readers on a journey of self-discovery and evolution. Through thought-provoking insights and actionable advice, they empower men to transcend outdated stereotypes and embrace a more inclusive and holistic vision of manhood.

Using surfing as a metaphor gives this book a unique grounding in the complexities of modern masculinity. Just as surfers must attune themselves to the rhythms of the ocean, so too must men learn to navigate the ever-changing currents of gender dynamics with grace and adaptability. In this analogy lies a profound truth: masculinity, like the ocean, is vast, dynamic, and ever-shifting—and it's up to each individual to ride the waves with skill and integrity.

As we stand at a crossroads in history, grappling with pressing social, cultural, and environmental challenges, the need for a new paradigm of masculinity has never been more urgent. "Making Good Men Great" is a beacon of hope in this sea of uncertainty—a guiding light for men who aspire to be positive contributors to a society striving for a more equitable and compassionate world.

As a father with a teenage son and daughter, I highly recommend this book. I have no doubt that readers will find in these pages not just inspiration but also practical tools and profound insights that will empower them to become better men and active participants in the ongoing evolution of masculinity.

Dr Mark Williams
    Professor of Cognitive Neuroscience
    Author of *The Connected Species*
    Founder of Brain Camp

Acknowledgments

This manuscript is the culmination of numerous individuals' guidance, support, and inspiration throughout our journey. Their collective wisdom has profoundly influenced our understanding of individuals' complex social and personal experiences across different eras and contexts.

First and foremost, we extend our heartfelt gratitude to Dr. Mark Williams, author of *The Connected Species* and our friend and collaborator. Our recent collaboration has been a source of profound inspiration and intellectual growth. His insights and unwavering support have enriched our personal and professional lives, and we look forward to our continued partnership.

We are deeply indebted to Mark Hodgson, whose mentorship has been a cornerstone of our development. His invaluable guidance has helped us navigate numerous challenges and encouraged us to prioritise the journey over pursuing perfection.

Our family, the bedrock of our lives, has been our unwavering foundation. To our children, Alexis and Tristan, whose growth into compassionate and empathetic individuals fills us with immense pride, and to our grandchildren, who bring boundless joy and wonder into our lives, we offer our deepest thanks.

Finally, we must express our most profound appreciation for each other. Our unwavering support and collaborative spirit have been fundamental to our achievements. In recognition of our significant contributions as authors and editors of this edition, we are honoured to share this journey. Our partnership has been a wellspring of inspiration and resilience, integral to our lives and this work.

Acknowledgments to the Bonfire Publishing Team

We are immensely grateful to the exceptional team at Bonfire Publishing for their unwavering support and dedication:

Miranda Spigener-Sapon, principal of the Bonfire team and our PR representative, has been crucial in promoting our work and vision through tireless advocacy and unmatched zeal.

DeVonna Prinzi, Co-Founder at Bonfire Cinema, whose editorial acumen and keen eye have refined this manuscript to its highest form.

Our talented cover designer is Jemi Koo, who has skillfully brought this book's visual essence to life.

Diamond Perkins, Molly Schinn, Corey Lee and Emilia Osborne, our meticulous editorial team, whose hard work and attention to detail have ensured the highest quality of this publication.

Thank you all for your invaluable contributions. This book, a testament to your expertise and dedication, stands as a shining example of the quality we have achieved together.

Introduction

Amongst the complexities of the modern world, it's essential that we recognise and honour the richness and diversity of masculinity. Like a distinct wave in the vast ocean, each man is a unique manifestation of the collective. If you have embarked on the journey of reading this book, chances are you are keen on becoming a better man. However, it is essential to clarify from the outset that I am not referring to material, political, or social success. True greatness is marked by character and integrity rather than material or social accomplishments.

Before we proceed any further, I suggest you take a moment and ask yourself a few pertinent questions:

Am I truly content and fulfilled?

Am I living according to core values?

Do I have a sense of purpose that has meaning beyond the material?

Am I living the life I genuinely desire?

Do I have healthy and meaningful relationships with the people who matter most to me?

Do I have aspirations that motivate me to keep learning and growing?

Am I struggling to comprehend my roles as a son, father, and husband?

Am I managing my work and personal life balance well?

Do I struggle to grasp what is expected of me as a man?

It's essential to take a step back and assess whether you're spending too much time at work and not enough on other essential aspects of your life. Ask yourself these questions, as the answer can make a big difference in your well-being, including helping you live longer. You are not alone if you're struggling to find the right balance, as this is a common experience in today's fast-paced world.

However, the problem is not just about managing your time well, being more productive or making the right choices. One of the most critical issues for men currently is that they feel burdened by the changing social expectations and changing gender roles that have evolved over the last few decades, leaving many men feeling lost.

My intention in writing this book is to help men find sustainable and practical answers to these questions. In doing so, we can then develop solutions to the various problems that men face so that they can chart their progress from being good men to being great men. I wanted to construct a guide that can aid men with the task of introspection and reflection on their lives, enabling them to recognise and address any obstacles hindering their progress.

I hope this guide is a valuable resource for any man looking to improve his relationships with himself and others in all aspects of life. Its practical tips, comprehensive approach, and detailed illustrations provide a roadmap to help men reach their full potential and lead fulfilling lives. It emphasises the importance of discovering one's true self, understanding and expressing emotions, effective communication, and building solid relationships. Additionally, the guide offers helpful advice for navigating the challenges of modern life.

To do this, we must examine masculine culture's traditional

ideologies and values and how they affect modern men's lives. To effectively address any problem, it is vital that we approach it from a multifaceted perspective. Understanding men and their behaviour requires us to take into account our cultural heritage and the current social context in which we exist. One valuable model that can aid in this endeavour is "Big History," which was developed by historian David Christian. This interdisciplinary field of study explores the history of the universe from the Big Bang to the present day, demonstrating the interconnectedness of various disciplines, such as cosmology, physics, chemistry, biology, anthropology, and history. Big History presents a comprehensive narrative that spans billions of years, providing a broader perspective on our cosmos that transcends traditional academic boundaries.

The fundamental concept underlying Big History is that we can better comprehend the past and present by integrating knowledge from numerous disciplines. It examines the significant thresholds and transitions in the history of the universe, such as the creation of galaxies, the emergence of life, the evolution of human beings, and the development of civilisations. It endeavours to identify patterns, trends, and commonalities across different time and space scales. It provides a broader context for understanding human history, promotes critical thinking skills, and fosters a deeper appreciation for the interconnectedness of all things.

By applying the Big History model to the study of men from the perspectives of biology, history, and psychology, we gain a more comprehensive understanding of what defines us as men. This approach also inspires a profound sense of wonder, curiosity, and reverence for the universe, highlighting the vast narrative of our existence and our role in the greater cosmic context. Ultimately, this perspective nurtures a deep appreciation for the interconnectedness of all things, as well as a sense of humility and gratitude for the diverse ecosystems that make up our planet.

Recognising that manhood extends beyond history, biology, and psychology is essential. The perception of masculinity and the significance attributed to being a man are deeply intertwined with social constructs. Central to this understanding is the concept of patriarchy, which is an influential ideology that has imprinted on our society in multifaceted ways. To delve into this matter comprehensively, a closer examination of the history of masculinity becomes imperative. Through this exploration, we gain deep insights into this ideology's profound impact on shaping our cultural norms and belief systems.

I am deeply passionate about men and masculinity, thanks to my discovery of the groundbreaking ideas of the first men's movement of the 1980s and psychologist Steven Biddulph's concepts that I came across over forty years ago. His ideas resonated with me, especially the importance of addressing social justice and equality concerns in our society. As a fellow psychologist, I am deeply troubled by the alarming mental health statistics among boys and men. Therefore, I firmly believe that it's crucial to continue the discourse on these issues and work towards a more equitable and just society for all. Over the years, many others have begun to tread similar paths; men who are passionate about understanding and improving the lives of men and society have started gathering. However, we have yet to become a movement.

Over the last few years, there has been a commendable effort to raise awareness among men of how traditional masculine

INTRODUCTION

roles and expectations have enabled the oppression of women. The objective is to help men better understand how their lives would be enriched by rethinking the ideas we had inherited from the patriarchal worldview that dominates our cultures. Unfortunately, some of the approaches taken to increase awareness have instead set up a divisive 'us vs them' mentality, which has left many men perplexed and misunderstood, leading to resentment.

Inclusivity is crucial when discussing masculinity if we want to bring about positive social change. As someone invested in this topic, it is essential that I share my perspective. I believe that men's struggles are not just personal but also collective, and understanding the social and cultural factors contributing to what is now called 'toxic masculinity' is vital. The ultimate goal of the effort to change how we think about masculinity is to empower men to create a more accepting and nurturing society. It's not about shaming or blaming men but rather dismantling harmful norms and creating equity for everyone.

Despite being published two decades ago, Steven Biddulph's book *Manhood* has insights into the problem of our concept of masculinity. Men's struggles still exist, and some may argue that things have worsened. As a psychologist who works closely with men on an individual level, I am aware of the complexity of this issue, requiring a thorough exploration of the individual's social context. Shedding light on this topic is imperative since the challenges men face extend beyond the personal level. Understanding the interplay of social and cultural influences contributing to our understanding of masculinity is essential. By doing so, we can work towards creating a society that embraces acceptance and nurturance for individuals.

This book is aimed at empowering men to become their best

selves. We have all been indoctrinated with rigid gender roles, but by acknowledging this fact, we can begin to dismantle harmful stereotypes and create a more equitable world. Over the past thirty years, my psychological practice has shifted towards serving men and boys, which is atypical since the majority of individuals seeking psychological assistance are women, and most psychologists are women.

It is typical for men to avoid seeking medical or emotional support. Still, I have noticed a fascinating trend where women started recommending me to their partners. Then, gradually, more men began seeking my psychological assistance without me having to advertise my services. Now, most of my clients are men ranging in age from thirteen to eighty. Many of these men and boys still hold onto traditional ideas and behaviours that prioritise male dominance. These beliefs, attitudes, and behaviours are still prevalent in our culture today and in traditional parenting practices. While extreme versions of this ideology are more commonly found in conservative circles, a subtler form of patriarchy can still have an influence, particularly for men who feel lost or lack purpose in their lives.

Certain religious groups have also contributed to reinforcing patriarchal ideas in recent decades because their own institutional processes and traditions have been developed within a strong patriarchal ideology. Then there are groups like the Men's Rights Movement, which aim to address issues they believe men face in a society changed by the last few decades' progress towards women's equality. They often argue that men face discrimination, oppression and violence, particularly in areas such as child custody, divorce, and criminal justice. It's important to acknowledge that some people hold views about gender that can be controversial and even harmful. However, it's also important to recognise that these views are often based on outdated and unproven ideas that experts in the field have rejected. Our focus should be on continuing to make progress in addressing inequality and creating a society that is inclusive and fair for everyone.

It seems highly unlikely that the Men's Movement has ever effectively helped men adapt to society's ever-changing dynamics. The evidence suggests that, in turn, men encounter a complex set of values, attitudes, beliefs, and expectations that leave them feeling overwhelmed and disoriented.

A clear discussion of the idea of biological determinism that underpins the very construct of patriarchal gender norms and roles is rarely mentioned, but it remains influential.

We have all been subject to the social pressure that tells us how to be a man. Often, our significant others expect us to conform to traditional stereotypes, which are further reinforced by sports clubs, politics, and religion. At the same time, they also expect us to be sensitive, caring, and nurturing. These conflicting messages can leave us feeling inadequate and incapable of building healthy relationships with those around us. To truly reach our full potential, it's important to redefine what it means to be a man. This involves challenging the traditional ideas of masculinity and men's roles that have been passed down for generations. We need to acknowledge our emotions and learn to communicate effectively with those around us. It's crucial to realise that vulnerability is not a weakness but a strength that helps us form deeper connections with others.

To illustrate what I mean about our society being influenced by patriarchy, I will tell a story from my life. I have lived in the Northern Beaches of Sydney since I was twelve and have always loved the ocean, so naturally, I took up surfing. In doing so, I learnt some life lessons about how our society works. For example, when I started surfing in the early '70s, no girls paddled out with us boys.

I heard from the older guys that during the early years of the first longboard era, women surfed along with men, and if you look at the history of surfing in Australia, you will find women right there at the beginning when the Duke came over from Hawaii. But something changed the attitudes of both girls and boys about who could, or more accurately should, surf. In the seventies, girls were expected to sit on the beach, look sexy in their bikinis and be intensely interested in every wave their boyfriend scored. They were expected to fawn over him when he returned to the beach. "Did you see that last one?" Girls learned to lie. "Yeah, I did," [gushing as expected].

Puberty Blues, a novel written by two teenage girls who had experienced the Australian beach culture, vividly portrayed the issue of gender inequality in surfing during the 1970s. Despite the ongoing discussions about Women's Liberation at the time, the male-dominated surf culture persisted, with boys claiming exclusive ownership of the waves and girls being relegated to the role of followers. The book shed light on the struggle of female surfers who desired to break free from social norms and compete with their male counterparts.

Apart from the differences between boys and girls, there were many other divisions that you had to navigate as a surfer. There was localism, where significant territoriality marked out who could surf what break, and a hierarchical valuing system about the surfboard you used. Your choice of equipment could lead to substantial bullying and division among surfers.

Another division was between those who surfed and the

'clubbies[1]' who exercised dominion over the small portion of the beach marked by red and yellow flags. These flags were often positioned right where the best waves broke. And this area was off-limits to surfboard riders. If you happened to surf into the flags, chances were that you lost your board, as the lifesavers confiscated it. This behaviour is imbued with patriarchal values like competitiveness and territoriality, as well as being acquisitive and preoccupied with status.

But not all of those who surf behave this way. Many hold to a different vision of surfing that speaks to the emotional experience, the aesthetics of this physical sport and the art of catching waves. It has a certain spirituality, much of which stemmed from Hawaii and the Aloha attitude that this traditional Hawaiian sport embodied. This approach to surfing is more aligned with an inclusive and companionable enjoyment of a shared activity.

The quintessential expression of this way of spending time with others pursuing the sport can be found in Shaun Tomson's "Surfers Code"[2006]. Shaun is a professional surfer who exemplifies a version of manhood based on character and integrity. *The Surfer's Code: 12 Simple Lessons for Riding through Life* emphasises respect, responsibility, and safety in the water and promotes a positive and inclusive surfing culture.

I am using surfing as an example of the way in which patriarchal ideology can take over and change the very nature of an experience. Like all human endeavours, surfing culture has positive values at its core and is susceptible to being co-opted. The pervasive influence of traditional masculinity has instilled a significant level of rigidity in our thinking and a reluctance

---

[1]

to adapt, both as individuals and as a society. This lesson is not exclusive to the realm of surfing and has implications for all facets of our lives, regardless of one's gender, race, religion, or ethnicity.

I believe that three core goals will enhance men's lives, and I will focus on these in this book:

Being the best man you can be in a relationship with yourself.

Being a great man in your relationships with others

Being a great leader in the company of men.

If we are going to meet the challenge and follow the example of men like Shaun Tomson, we need to change. Becoming a great man means learning a new code and framework that allows men to be more responsive, flexible and resilient.

1

Traditional Masculinity

The Time Has Come

I know many honourable men brimming with the desire to excel for their own sake and that of their families. Some of these men also aspire to leave a positive mark in their professional spheres and, occasionally, within broader society. The challenge lies in discovering a suitable pathway in which to fulfil these noble aspirations and enable men to flourish in a world that no longer provides universally approved pathways to success. Rapid changes in how our society functions at a fundamental level have left many of us unclear about what is expected of us as men.

Before we can even begin to find our way forward, we, as men, need to understand the roots of our difficulties. This is why I am constantly pulled towards investigating our beliefs about what we consider to be the very essence of men. Who, indeed, are we? What factors contribute to our specific behaviours and tendencies? Why are we wrestling with internal conflicts and relational turmoil? Why are so many of us more depressed, anxious and psychologically distressed? What propels us towards a tragic path, leading to a suicide rate higher than that of women? These questions underline the urgency of our understanding of the complex nature of men's struggles.

Given the relative affluence, security, and safety we enjoy, especially in the Western World, our psychological and emotional struggles are particularly puzzling. It's disheartening to see the state of men's physical and mental health in developed nations. Looking at the numbers, it becomes evident why we urgently need to address men's health issues. Men have a higher mortality rate than women in many developed countries, primarily due to preventable causes such as cardiovascular disease and accidents. The World Health Organisation tells us that globally, men have significantly higher suicide rates than women.

On top of that, men often face challenges when seeking mental health support. The pressure to conform to social expectations and traditional ideas of masculinity makes it harder for men to discuss their feelings openly and seek the support they need. It's hard to believe that even after all the scrutiny from both women and men over the past half-century, the stereotypes surrounding masculinity and patriarchal norms still hold such a firm grip on men's attitudes and behaviours, just like they did in our ancestors' time.

These lingering stereotypes and deeply rooted social norms create a harmful cycle. They take a toll on men's emotional well-being, discourage seeking help when needed, and worsen mental health issues. It's crucial for us to challenge and dismantle these harmful ideals collectively. We must ask ourselves why these archaic norms persist and what barriers prevent men from evolving beyond these dated perspectives.

We must foster a culture that embraces men's vulnerabilities and strengths, encourages self-care, and promotes seeking support when necessary. We can do this by opening up the conversation to raise our awareness and provide accessible resources tailored to men's unique needs and working towards creating a healthier and more compassionate society for people of all genders.

The men who come to see me are unusual only in one way. They are looking for something better, more significant and healthier. Unsure of what they seek, they have often lost themselves in addictions like work or sport, or worse, alcohol, drugs and gambling. Frequently urged on by their partners, and now more commonly, other men who have seen me, they have taken a step the majority of men are still reluctant to take. They have come to ask for assistance. Aside from feelings of anxiety, depression, and pain from relationships gone wrong, most are in what can be best described as an existential crisis. It is that time when we confront the very meaning of our life, its purpose, and its value. It is, for many, a distressing time. Who am I? What's it all about? Do I want to do what I do, and is that of any value?

From the moment we first draw breath, we are conditioned to perceive the world through the prism of 'masculinity. Once this notion of manhood becomes deeply entrenched, we often define ourselves by what we do. We identify ourselves by our professions and occupations. 'I'm a builder,' one might say, or 'I'm a surgeon.' Another integral component of our identity is our sense of belonging. This could be traced to our ethnicity, religion, chosen profession, or even a particular sports team allegiance.

In an era where the conventional notions of masculinity are being upended and reimagined, today's men find themselves at a crossroads. They are compelled to scrutinise their roles within a rapidly changing society and often confront transformative ideas and beliefs that significantly affect their self-identity. However, what are the consequences when these anchors of our sense of who we are and who we are supposed to be become fluid? What lies beyond that moment of uncertainty?

Like many navigating the vast ocean of knowledge in our digital age, my initial foray into research was led by the omnipresent beacon of the internet. I turned to Google, that modern oracle of information. Despite some reservations about its accuracy, Wikipedia proved to be a fertile ground of information, providing a suitable starting point for my preliminary overview. My exploration started with a deep dive into feminism. Why? Because I knew that feminism has a solid academic tradition. The Second Wave of Feminism in the 1970s was part of the social and civil rights movement for the emancipation and equality of all members of the community. It inspired those women already situated in academia to pursue questions about patriarchy and its influence on women's roles and lives. This has led to a trove of insightful and intellectually rigorous perspectives about human society and how gender roles have impacted both sexes.

Anticipating an equally rigorous and in-depth analysis of Masculinity, I was disappointed to find in my initial investigation that there was no similar comprehensive approach to the issue of masculinity. The content of what was on offer failed to provide an insightful and informative analysis. Rather than an in-depth analysis of masculinity to answer that age-old question of 'what does it mean to be a man, or what makes a good man?' the question being asked is 'What is wrong with men'? The focus was on men's shortcomings, symptoms or disorders within a recurring theme that men are damaged.

The feminist challenge to the concept of biological determinism, which underpins patriarchal descriptions and prescriptions of gender stereotypes, had only been loosely applied to men. Whereas there had been a robust analysis of how this had negatively impacted women and their way of being in the world, the discussion of patriarchy's influence on men was extremely limited.

So, as we delve deeper into the subject of men, we must engage in critical thinking and a constructive dialogue beyond superficial discussions about men's shortcomings. The question "what is wrong with men?" has shaped much of the research and dialogue around masculinity. The question of why the concept of masculinity that was socially accepted only a few decades ago is now seen as damaged has not been subjected to thorough investigation.

As it stands today, two principal areas of study emerge as paramount. The first is based on a biological and psychological perspective, focusing on the innate characteristics and traits of the male identity. One of the concerning observations in the discourse surrounding men's issues is the tendency to view men's suffering through the lens of pathology. This approach suggests an inherent biological disposition to men's struggles that exists independently of the social and situational factors that contribute to them. According to this viewpoint, the obstacles to men's well-being stem from some pathological or deviant process, whether genetically determined or linked to individual psychopathology. Essentially, men's suffering is portrayed as a manifestation of mental illness.

This perspective is problematic for several reasons. Firstly, it stigmatises men experiencing difficulties by framing their struggles as indicative of a broader pathology. This discourages men from seeking help or support, as they feel ashamed or embarrassed about their perceived mental health issues. Furthermore, pathologising men's issues in this way obscures the social and environmental factors that contribute to their struggles. Focusing solely on individual pathology, we risk overlooking the broader structural issues contributing to men's mental health, such as social isolation, economic insecurity, and cultural expectations around masculinity and emotional expression.

In order to address men's mental health issues effectively, it is essential to move beyond a narrow pathologised perspective and consider the broader social and situational factors that contribute to men's struggles. It is critical to remember that men, like everyone else, are more than the sum of their supposed pathologies or their socio-political circumstances. Each man is a unique reflection of his experiences, beliefs and perceptions, which requires a broader, more nuanced understanding of his nature extending beyond simplistic ideas such as pathology.

The second school takes a more socio-political approach, examining the issues of equity and distributive justice amongst men and emphasises the problems that lead to the marginalisation of some men in our communities. This area of study looks at the bigger picture of power, socioeconomic advantage and disadvantage, and how this impacts men and their overall well-being. However, this more political approach fails to address the fundamental question of the complexity of our understanding of the idea of masculinity.

These two perspectives alone cannot fully capture that complexity. There is a growing need to re-envision our understanding of what it means to be a man, starting from the ground up. By developing an integrative framework that considers all aspects of male identity, we can better understand masculinity and work towards a more equitable society for all.

To truly understand the complexities of human behaviour and interactions, we must look beyond surface-level explanations of individual problems or dysfunctions. Instead, we must take a broad and integrated approach, drawing on insights from various disciplines. History can offer us a rich tapestry of human experience, revealing patterns and trends that have shaped our world over time. Anthropology can help us appreciate the incredible diversity of human cultures and societies, highlighting commonalities and differences that inform our sense of self and otherness. Sociology can give us a deeper understanding of how social structures and institutions shape our lives, from family and community to government and economy. Psychology can shed light on the inner workings of our minds and emotions, revealing the complex interplay of thoughts, feelings, and behaviours that drive our actions. And the biological sciences can help us decode the intricate genetic and physiological factors that influence our health, development, and behaviour. By weaving together these different strands of knowledge, we can better understand what it means to be human and how we can create a more just and harmonious world for all.

The systemic ideological view is a perspective that closely aligns with feminist thought. It emphasises the importance of examining the broader social structures and systems that contribute to issues of inequality and oppression. This view recognises that larger cultural forces shape individual actions and beliefs, and seeks to identify and challenge how these systems perpetuate discrimination and marginalisation. For example, a systemic ideological approach to analysing gender inequality might involve examining how traditional gender roles are reinforced through media, education, and other cultural institutions and how we can work towards dismantling these structures to create a more equitable society. Overall, the systemic ideological view emphasises the interconnectedness of different social issues and the need for collective action to create lasting change.

Ultimately, I am arguing for an approach that integrates the dispositional, situational and systemic factors that influence men individually and collectively. This is crucial if we are to foster a more profound understanding of men and masculinity to assist men in evolving from a modus operandi that is failing men and society as a whole. To steer this transformative journey, we must pose a new question that seeks to inspire rather than pathologise. 'What constitutes a Great Man?'

Fortunately, in recent years, there has been a greater emphasis on the academic exploration of masculinity and how it may be represented in historical narratives of social struggles, in a philosophy of masculinity and its impact on sociology, and a psychology specific to masculinity. And most of that came from women, which, unfortunately, often did not get much traction in the various boys' clubs that exist in our society.

Wait, what boys' clubs, you ask? Unfortunately, there are very few political movements that are not marred by elements of misogyny. Before you dismiss the idea, accept that an honest appraisal of human history must acknowledge that men have been in charge of society and its institutions and used law and cultural narratives to ensure that the vast majority of societies around the world have been, and still are, male-centred.

Allow me to add a caveat. There is no question that in yesteryears, the domains of philosophy, politics, history, science, and business were predominantly male-dominated. But behind the veil, as much as they could, some women forged a foothold into the male-dominated fields of the sciences, philosophy and arts. But it was done on the sly and only by those whose access was due to their position as wives and daughters of privileged men. Women feared the reprisals that could, and at times did, cause them immense harm. Patriarchal thinking was laden with myths about the inherent abilities of men and women, creating a divisive and exclusive environment that neither men nor women challenged without risk.

Ultimately, women were compelled to embrace radical action, to unite and spark a dialogue that fostered transformation. Achieving recognition as independent legal entities rather than mere extensions of men, securing the right to vote, accessing professions previously barred to them, and acquiring economic independence, were all rights won through fierce battles. Women were incarcerated, tortured and killed in their struggle for emancipation, much like slaves. While this mission remains an ongoing endeavour, these social shifts have significantly recalibrated the balance of power and control in Western societies.

Men, for their part, have yet to adjust to these changes fully. But that is not surprising. Over thousands of years, the description of manhood has been one of dominance and control. Even the least important man in the hierarchy of society was in control in his home. This new acknowledgement that the women in our lives are adults who have their own agency demands that we reassess our understanding of our own agency. On one hand, it lets us off the hook of having to be responsible for everyone, but on the other hand, it leaves us with unanswered questions about how to respond to a whole set of new expectations.

In this era of significant transformation, men stand at an intriguing cultural intersection. Like thespians abruptly conscious of the shortcomings in their script, men are beckoned to improvise, to reframe their roles in a freshly envisioned performance. The curtain has risen on a novel narrative of masculinity that respectfully acknowledges its past without being anchored to it. It must be a narrative attuned to the realities of the present and thoughtful of the future.

Yet, let me underscore this with absolute passion: this does not mean we should strive to emulate women. That would be a misguided endeavour. The notion of androgyny is a flawed concept that has been rightfully sidelined. As men, we must adhere to the inherent differences that fundamentally define us. It is crucial that we not only comprehend this uniqueness but that we also refine it to be able to live in complementary relationships with women.

Each individual, whether man or woman, serves as an indispensable character in the grand drama of life, each contributing their distinct strengths, viewpoints, and experiences to this magnificent tableau. The metamorphosis of masculinity does not require a wholesale renunciation of inherent traits; rather, it necessitates a redefinition that upholds our fundamental essence while fostering a broader spectrum of expression and understanding. This dual challenge and opportunity is the mantle now entrusted to contemporary man.

This enterprise necessitates involvement from men across all strata of life. It is not a monologue to be dominated by a singular voice nor a discourse driven by one ideological standpoint. The effort should traverse disciplines, cultures, and communities, echoing how feminism revolutionised our understanding of equality, property rights, sexuality, and violence.

The hour has come for men to unite with women, participating in a global movement to better humanity. To redefine masculinity is not to dilute it but to distil its essence, enrich its character, and broaden its scope. The time for this endeavour is now, as we strive to weave a richer tapestry of human existence in which every thread—every man—contributes to a brighter, more inclusive future.

As we tumble and whirl through the dance of life, we must realise that past assumptions of male dominance have no place in shaping our future. We can create new patterns, rhythms, and ways of being that celebrate the individual wave and the vast ocean of our collective existence. It is time we cast aside outdated scripts and write a new narrative that genuinely appreciates the full spectrum of being a man.

2

I want to raise the bar. I want Good Men to become Great!

How are we, men, doing?

Okay, here's the deal: we need to discuss 'masculinities' because there is more than one way to be a man. It's time to ditch those old-school stereotypes and look at things differently. Why? Because we've got some serious work to do to be better men.

I frequently encounter and address sensitive topics in my work with boys and men. These include attachment issues, behavioural issues, impulse control issues, body image issues, identity issues, and relationship issues. Each area requires careful and compassionate attention, and I strive to provide helpful, fair, and safe support to those I work with. Whether supporting someone through a difficult period of self-discovery or helping them navigate complex relationship dynamics, my aim is always to create a welcoming and supportive environment where individuals can feel heard and valued.

Remember, life's hard, or at least some of it is as hard as you make it. All of us will experience difficulties in our lives, and they will manifest in various ways. These issues often stem from various factors, including how men were raised, changes in gender roles and expectations, and shifts in life expectancy that impact later life. Unfortunately, there is still a great need for greater awareness and understanding of men's struggles.

One of the reasons for this is that men tend not to openly discuss their health and how they're feeling. Additionally, many men hesitate to take action when they're not feeling physically or mentally well, which can exacerbate problems. This is further compounded by the fact that men often engage in risky activities that threaten their health, and there is a significant stigma surrounding mental health among men in particular.

All of these factors can make it challenging for men to seek the help and support they need, which is why it's so important to raise awareness and encourage open dialogue around these issues. Doing so can help break down these barriers and ensure men feel empowered to care for their physical and mental health.

The first Young and Well National Survey [2013], a scientific study of young men from across Australia, identified alarming statistics that suggest we are especially failing young men:

The levels of drug and alcohol use and abuse amongst young men have increased, and those levels of use are being sustained over a more extended period of their lives.

Nearly one in five young men in the past 12 months have felt that life is hardly worth living.

Almost one in ten young men have thought about taking their own life.

Unemployment and moderate to very high levels of psychological distress lead to suicidal thoughts and behaviour.

Forty-two per cent of young men are experiencing psychological distress.

For every woman who commits suicide, three men die by their own hand.

A study conducted on students aged seven to twelve found that many boys reported feeling constantly stressed and unable to overcome difficulties. Specifically, thirty per cent of boys reported feeling this way. Additionally, more than half of the boys had low levels of resilience. Of those who lacked resilience, forty-three per cent believed that violence was an acceptable way to solve relationship issues.

Further analysis showed that a third of the boys surveyed drank at dangerous levels. Shockingly, one in four lacked the confidence to say no to unwanted sexual experiences, while 16 per cent felt it was necessary to carry a weapon. In addition, one in ten students from schools surveyed in Victoria, Queensland, SA and NSW had gambled in the past year.

These findings highlight that many young men lack fundamental skills such as impulse control, conflict resolution, and relationship-building. These skills are essential for coping with life's challenges, particularly social pressures. Parents, schools, and communities must urgently provide support and resources to help boys develop these skills and navigate the complexities of modern life.

According to a recent study in Germany, seventy-one per cent of young men aged between eighteen and thirty-five believe they must solve personal problems without asking for help. Half of the respondents (fifty-one per cent) feel weak and vulnerable when they show emotion and fifty-three per cent are uncomfortable talking about their feelings. In addition, fifty per cent of the participants admit to ignoring health problems, assuming they will go away on their own. Furthermore, sixty per cent of them sometimes feel sad, lonely, or isolated.

Physical appearance plays a significant role for the respondents, with fifty-nine per cent stating that they put a lot of effort into having a sporty and muscular body. Fifty-five per cent agree with the statement that their appearance and demeanour show that they are a real man. In contrast, forty-eight per cent of respondents feel disturbed when men show their gayness in public, and forty-two per cent admit that men who appear effeminate or feminine to them "sometimes get a joke" from them.

Regarding risk and competition, the study shows that sixty-three per cent of young men often strive competitively to be among those they consider to be 'the best'. Forty-three per cent admit to liking to drive aggressively and quickly, while forty-two per cent agree with the statement, "Sometimes I drink so much alcohol that I don't know anymore what I did."

Regarding heterosexual relationships, fifty-two per cent of young men see their role as earning enough money at work to fund the household. At the same time, their partner is primarily responsible for housework. Additionally, forty-nine per cent believe it is essential that they, as the male, have the final say in decisions in a relationship or marriage. Meanwhile, thirty-nine per cent of young men would like their partner to put her own needs or interests on hold and prioritise his, seeing this as their partner supporting them. Only forty per cent of those surveyed would take parental leave for longer than a few weeks.

Attitudes towards women and sexuality are also revealed in the study. Half of the men surveyed (fifty per cent) do not want to be in a relationship with a woman with many past sexual partners. In comparison, thirty-seven per cent admit to being tempted to sleep with as many women as possible. According to forty-seven per cent of the men surveyed, provocative behaviour on the part of women can be understood as an invitation. Additionally, forty-one per cent feel it is their right to compliment women, look at them in an evaluating manner, and whistle at them.

The study also found that more than a third of the men surveyed (thirty-four per cent) physically abuse women to make them respect them. For every third man (thirty-three per cent), it is acceptable if he occasionally slaps his partner with his hand during an argument.

Despite the majority of the men surveyed (eighty-eight per cent) being at peace with themselves and their image of men and believing they are the way a man should be, ninety-five per cent feel pressure to change. Fifty-four per cent are willing to develop themselves because of this pressure, while thirty-eight per cent would like to be left alone in this regard.

Lastly, the study reveals that seventy-seven per cent of the women surveyed have significantly higher expectations of men than men have of themselves. They believe that every man should now know what behaviour is expected of him when it comes to equality. One in four (twenty-five per cent) expect men to forego their historical male (power) privileges. In comparison, almost as many (twenty-six per cent) agree with the proposition that men find it difficult to understand their (new) role, and twenty-one per cent of those women believe it is necessary to help men find a new path in a changed world.

As a psychologist, I have avoided labelling what boys and men face as illnesses or abnormalities. Instead, I approach these issues as different states of being that individuals may encounter. My primary concern is the emotional and cognitive processes, as well as the behaviours, that males exhibit within their social environment. However, the notion of identity, which is often disregarded, is a crucial element at the heart of these challenges. Examining how one's sense of self influences our experiences and interactions with the world around us is essential to understanding and addressing these complex issues fully.

So, then, are men bad, ill or just lost? Let me explain where I'm coming from in this context. A disease or illness primarily pertains to the physical brain, not the mind's realm. A disease can damage the grey matter and the neurological network—the 'hardware'—which can indeed impact the mind. Yet, when we discuss problems of the mind, we refer to the mental activity produced by this brain—the 'software,' if you will. For those who might dismiss this as a subtle quibble, let me assure you that this distinction is far from trivial. It lays the groundwork for understanding why men are in a state of crisis within an existential context.

In an existential crisis, we find ourselves at a profound crossroads, forced to reckon with the very foundations of our being, the significance of our existence, and the alignment of our lives with our deepest values. This existential turmoil is what many boys—and, I emphasise, boys—as well as men wrestle with, often leading to psychological discomfort that an underlying disorder can intensify.

Our objective, therefore, shouldn't be merely to confront these conditions as pathologies waiting to be eradicated. Instead, we must appreciate them as beacons illuminating a deeper, more profound internal struggle. They represent calls for help from the abyss of an existential crisis—urgent pleas for empathy, connection, and a reshaping of identity. To truly support men and boys in traversing the complex maze of their psyche, we need to address these foundational concerns.

I wish to underscore this point: The issues plaguing men extend beyond the realm of psychological disorders or mental illnesses. The heart of the matter lies in the psychological distress emerging from an outdated cultural, political and religious ideology of manhood that no longer serves us. It's about confronting our understanding of existence, ethics, and morality. While it's true that some men grapple with psychological disorders or mental health issues, these often act as overlays, adding complexity to the fundamental issue—the outmoded paradigm of masculinity. Embedded in our cultural fabric's warp and weft, this paradigm calls for a thorough and careful deconstruction.

In essence, we can conclude that our physical well-being falls short of what it could be, our psychological adaptability and endurance are lacking, our social connections are not as aligned as they should be, and we need a greater sense of direction, significance, and determination in our daily lives.

The bottom line is that we are surviving... but not thriving.

3

So, how did we get into this mess?

Engulfed in a ceaseless torrent of social and technological transformations, our society is losing touch with the very essence of what makes us human. Every time a new piece of technology comes out, we're told it will improve our lives. But honestly, many of them don't live up to the hype. Take the Digital Revolution, for example. It was supposed to be this huge game-changer, but did it really deliver on all those promises? I'm not so sure. With all the amazing advancements in technology, it can be easy to forget what makes us human. Sometimes, technology can make us feel more isolated instead of helping us connect with each other.

The mission before us is no less than this: to seamlessly weave these technological advancements into the fabric of our lives while ensuring that our fundamental humanity—those essential attributes that constitute our very being—remains unblemished and intact.

Throughout history, there have been many new ideas that seemed like positive changes at first but ended up causing harm to society and individuals over time. These consequences can be quite severe, and we still deal with them today. Eventually, we may have to consider whether the costs of progress are too high. As the author Aldous Huxley once said, 'Time Must Have a Stop'.

In today's world, the rate of change is rapid, with ever-increasing amounts of information being uploaded into our lives and needing to be assessed as to how it impacts us as individuals. Many people, men and women, are feeling overwhelmed by the sense that the goalposts are constantly moving, and they feel that it is a struggle to keep up with this constant change and the demand that we adapt. There are significant and complex issues with both natural and human-designed environments that are impacting all of us. A prime example of this decline can be seen in our sperm count, which is one measure of our masculinity. Modern men produce less sperm than their ancestors did a century ago, and the quality of this reproductive material is also decreasing. We find ourselves at a turning point in history. As Marcel Proust once said, "The real journey of discovery is not about finding new places, but about seeing things with new eyes."

Right now, we need to look at masculinity in a new way that fits with the world we live in today. We have to be willing to re-evaluate the assumptions and attitudes that were developed in the ancient world and that reflect the patriarchal belief that biology should determine the rights and responsibilities of individual humans. Let's get real here. We no longer drive chariots, use oil lamps or believe that slavery is morally right. The model of manhood that has remained entrenched in human societies over the millennia is no more workable in the twenty-first century than using papyrus in our offices. The old-fashioned ideas that men should be in charge of the world are no longer either acceptable or workable. These ideas of dominance, not just over women but incorporated into class systems as well as racist ideology, have quite rightly been challenged and found to be morally untenable.

Our evolution away from these ideas means that we need to have a more open and honest conversation about what masculinity really means. It's like when scientists realised that their old ideas were not working and they needed to come up with new ones. We are at a similar point where we need to change our old ideas about masculinity and come up with new ones that work better for everyone. We need a masculinity that fits with a world where all humans are seen to have equal worth and are valued for who they are as individuals, not for belonging to a particular sex, race, or class.

When women challenged the traditional stereotype of womanhood and how it had been used to subjugate and disempower them over thousands of years, they opened up an area of study that has been pursued by academics in many universities. Unfortunately, there was no acknowledgement that traditional stereotypes of manhood should also be rigorously studied. The easy answer is that Universities are patriarchal institutions. And yes, this is true. But, the fact that these institutional ideas of masculinity are based on ancient and long-held gender stereotypes that harm both men and women is a new insight. It was only a couple of decades ago that we were still being fed flawed and socially regressive ideas like those promoted in the book "Men are from Mars, Women are from Venus."

In these extreme perspectives, we find the echoes of Jean-Jacques Rousseau's 'Emile' and Simone de Beauvoir's 'The Second Sex', two works that, in their own time, fundamentally challenged or perpetuated prevailing notions of gender. Yet, their stark differentiation of the sexes oversimplifies the complex interplay of biology, culture, and individual identity. However, the opposite belief that men and women are essentially the same is also flawed.

Each perspective is an unsophisticated caricature that overlooks the intricate tapestry of socially constructed gender identities and the lived experiences of all humans. It dismisses the countless ways individuals might embody elements of what is described as masculinity and femininity, instead reinforcing a binary, reductionist view of the concept of gender.

Our task is to shift the conversation from these extremes and embrace a more nuanced view that allows for a broad spectrum of identities and recognises and celebrates the rich diversity of human expression. We must foster a dialogue that respects both the similarities and distinctions among humans and acknowledges the multifaceted ways in which we all embody our identities.

We need a richer, deeper dialogue that considers the similarities and differences between the human characteristics allocated to the two traditionally sex-determined genders, embracing a spectrum of identities rather than forcing them into outdated, restrictive boxes. Only then can we truly grapple with the question of what it means to be a man in the contemporary world.

While our past brims with rigid delineations of gender roles, buttressed by the imposing edifice of patriarchy, our present reality reflects a more nuanced landscape. Gender, as Simone de Beauvoir once sagely asserted in 'The Second Sex', is not a biological fact but a social construct, a grand narrative sculpted over millennia that assigns meanings to the physiological differences between men and women. This narrative, wielded by patriarchal societies worldwide, codified a spectrum of stereotypes around masculinity and femininity.

Through the dogged perseverance of women and their allies, age-old female gender constructs have been assiduously dismantled, engendering a seismic shift in our conceptualisation of gender. Echoing Judith Butler's groundbreaking notion in 'Gender Trouble', gender is no longer perceived as an unchanging identity but rather as a performance, a daily enactment that moulds our individual personhood. This pivotal redirection has ushered in an era of both disconcerting ambiguity and liberating potential for the conceptualisation of gender. No longer do men and women have to conform to ideas about who they are as humans based solely on their biological sex.

This has led to a dismantling of the social and legal inequalities that were based on these concepts, which has led to some confusion in our understanding of the concept of equality. In the shadow of these seismic changes, a particular concept remains influential. The idea that equates equality with sameness. This flawed interpretation is a remnant of the original philosophical arguments about the equality of persons, which has been robustly disputed as appropriate for the conceptualisation of equality amongst humans. This misreading of the feminist endeavour suggests a world scrubbed clean of all biological or sexual distinctions, paving the way towards an androgynous landscape bereft of difference. However, as Audre Lorde elucidates in 'Sister Outsider,' "It is not our differences that divide us. It is our inability to recognise, accept, and celebrate those differences." Therefore, equality does not require homogeneity but rather the acknowledgement and respect of our multifaceted identities.

Equally problematic is the erroneous belief that the liberation from these patriarchal constructs implies that the gender problem has been solved. Once the stereotypes are demolished, belief in gender as a valid description of sex difference will cease to be a battlefield. However, as Michel Foucault elaborated in 'The History of Sexuality', power structures are deeply embedded and continually shape our understanding of gender and sexuality. Thus, dismantling traditional constructs is just the beginning of a much larger project to create a society that truly honours and respects the full spectrum of human identity.

The idea behind the equality project was born from the belief that everyone should be valued equally, regardless of their possessions, social status, or family background. It was not about being the same as everyone else but about being recognised as equally valuable human beings. This meant that you deserved respect and dignity regardless of who you were or where you came from. For example, a person who lives in poverty should be afforded the same basic human rights as someone who is wealthy. The goal was to create a society where everyone was treated fairly and justly, regardless of their circumstances.

Throughout history, biological differences between men and women have been exploited as a means to subjugate women and deny them self-determination. As women challenged the preconceived ideas that dictated their place in society, they and their supporters were able to demonstrate that biological sex differences do not determine character, intelligence or a capacity to live one's life as an autonomous individual. This has led some to doubt that there is any significance to the differing biological nature of women and men. However, advocating for the insignificance of these differences may unintentionally eliminate a fundamental aspect of our lived human experiences. It is important to acknowledge and address these differences in a way that celebrates diversity and promotes equality rather than perpetuating a system of oppression.

The challenge lies not in obliterating these differences but in a nuanced understanding of their implications, just as biologist and gender theorist Anne Fausto-Sterling advocates in 'Sexing the Body'. Our goal should be to acknowledge our differences while maintaining that they do not dictate our inherent worth.

The shift in the legal landscape to acknowledge women as equals to men has led some to believe that the issue of gender stereotyping has been conclusively addressed. Yet, the lived reality presents a stark contrast. The enduring influence of traditional constructs of masculinity, and for that matter, femininity, continues to permeate all of our lives, creating confusion and cognitive dissonance between the traditional manner in which so many of us are still raised and the expectations of modern society. It is important to acknowledge that the reimagining of ourselves within this new paradigm is an ongoing project. Thousands of years of tradition cannot be swept away in a few decades. And it won't happen automatically.

Two polarised archetypes have emerged from this cultural churning. The first is the successful yet emotionally detached man, echoing the eponymous protagonist in F. Scott Fitzgerald's 'The Great Gatsby', admired yet disparaged for his pursuit of material success at the expense of nurturing relationships. The second archetype offers a foil: the less competitive man, deemed to be 'in touch with his feminine side', and very often subjected to mockery for embracing traits traditionally associated with femininity. These conflicting expectations create an existential quandary for many men, a labyrinthine trap where every turn seems to lead to criticism, eventually driving many to retreat into silence.

Moreover, in the midst of this identity crisis, toxic traits often misattributed to manhood—bullying, reckless aggression, unbridled greed, relentless politicking—continue to cast a long, troubling shadow, as noted by sociologist Michael Kimmel in 'Angry White Men.' These traits are not inherent aspects of masculinity, they are instead distortions amplified by social expectations. In response, we've seen attempts to offer alternative models of masculinity, but many of these amount to merely 'feminising' masculine traits, which, while well-intentioned, often fail to address the root of the issue: the need for a comprehensive reimagining of what it means to be a man in the modern world.

It's clear that men, and our understanding of what it means to be a man, faces challenges because patriarchal stereotypes remain a dominant influence within all areas of our lives and our social institutions. Despite the insights into what it is to be a human that psychology, anthropology, history, sociology, and, more recently, neuroscience have provided us over the last few decades, men are still struggling to see themselves outside of these traditional and unhelpful characterisations.

4

The Iron Age Warrior in the Digital Age

Here's a quick quiz:

Are you possessive? That can be over a person or persons, property, ideas, etc.

Are you conscious of your status? Keen to climb the career ladder to enjoy the power that it brings?

Do you tend to look at what you own as a mark of who you are and your value?

Are you competitive? Especially against others.

Do you see life as a series of battles that must be fought and won?

If the answer is 'yes' to one or more of these questions, then there is a good chance that you are, as a man, patriarchal. This is because you are conforming to the social norm for men.

What's Patriarchy? Patriarchy is an entrenched, overarching, ideologically based system of beliefs and assumptions about human nature and how we should run our communities. Although it is an important aspect of the ideology, "patriarchy is generally not an explicit ongoing effort by men to dominate women. It is a long-standing system we are born into and participate in, mostly unconsciously." [Daily Kos.]

In fact, patriarchy is part of the very fabric of our social, religious and political institutions, having been the driving ideology of our society and civilisation for thousands of years. It is useful to remember that the patriarch is the man who is the head of the clan, tribe or other political unit such as a nation. The idea of men being the head of the household is an example of the way the power of one man, the chief or the king, is filtered down to the lives of ordinary men.

Breaking down complex academic language into simpler terms can be extremely helpful, especially when discussing concepts like patriarchy. Through my experiences studying and working with people, I've found that patriarchy is built on four main ideas: wanting to control a specific area, having a clear hierarchy, prioritising acquiring things, and being competitive. These aren't just abstract ideas but things that impact our personal identity, relationships, social interactions, and professional lives. The description of the valuable characteristics of a good man has changed little over the millennia, and the Iron Age Warrior is an embodiment of those characteristics. Strength, power and determination, fearless and relentless, always seeking to win, seeing life as a competition for power [hierarchy], wealth [acquisition], and territory.

But how do these characteristics fit into the modern world?

Many people still view life as a battle where they either win or lose. Winning means getting material possessions, social status, and power. Losing leads to feelings of shame, inadequacy, and vulnerability. This kind of thinking can cause anxiety and make people feel like they need to constantly improve themselves. It's like a condition called "affluenza," which makes people feel envious, regretful, and ashamed for not being what society tells them to be: ambitious, acquisitive, competitive, and financially affluent. So, let's look at how these attitudes and beliefs create problems for the men of today.

This modern warrior archetype is still fixated on physical strength, attractiveness to others, and impressing people in power. In the past, people pursued these goals by mastering weapons, fighting, and taking what they wanted. Nowadays, people go to the gym and participate in sports. It's not uncommon to see young boys in their teenage years spending a lot of time and money building muscle and losing body fat as if they were preparing for battle.

The pursuit of female attention remains, in many ways, unchanged. As the biological drive for sex kicks in, the adolescent boy starts to seek connection and sex within the accepted ideals of his cultural group. In just about all societies, a boy's social stature depends on his ability to secure attractive female companionship. Any evidence - real or fabricated - of such relationships can propel a young man up the social ladder. Thus, sex becomes a compulsive fixation, overlayed by competitive and acquisitive ideals that are performative rather than connective. Added to this, many boys' idea of what sex actually looks like is often informed by the lurid and unrealistic depictions found in online pornography, which even adult men might have found difficult to access a few decades ago.

Despite the progress made by feminism, women are still often seen as objects that belong to men, even in Western society. They are valued for the status they bring to their male partners, in a similar way to how ancient warriors used to show off their trophies. It's like we've traded the skin of a sabre-toothed tiger for a quick like on Instagram - a good comparison for our digital age - but the core of this issue remains unchanged. We think we have evolved, but our actions still reflect the same ideas of male dominance that have been present throughout history.

As our digital age warrior steps into adulthood, his markers of triumph become located in his choice of occupation, wealth and popularity. Alcohol and drugs that are initially just for partying become his refuge and his claim to fame as he grapples with his dread of being inadequate, the fear of rejection, the terror of abandonment, and the horror of isolation—feelings that will shadow him for a lifetime. He prepares himself for his subsequent existential crisis: the looming spectre of adult responsibility. What used to be the simple act of leaving the nest and caring for oneself has morphed into a formidable challenge due to the expectations of our materialistic and status-driven society.

Having gained a semblance of independence, he next confronts the challenge of transitioning into the roles of partner and parent. His solution, traditionally justified by his role as provider, is to be absent physically, immersing himself in work with little time spared for relationships. He also emotionally retains his guard, frightened of displaying vulnerability in his relationship with his partner.

A growing sense of dissatisfaction with his choices or a sense of loneliness may spark introspection, yet all too frequently, he poses the wrong question. He ponders whether he desires to stay in this relationship, vacillating on the brink of commitment. Instead of contemplating departure, he would do better to ask, 'How can I improve within this relationship?' This pattern illustrates his ambivalence towards the emotional work required to sustain relationships, hinting at the archaic influences of patriarchal paradigms.

Ultimately, heading into older age, this persistent vacillation leads him into the gloomy realms of clinical anxiety and depression. Rather than seeking a resolution to his quandary, he leans on medications that offer inconsistent relief. He is left with a lingering sense of failure whether he stays or departs. Children, if they're part of his world, pose another conundrum. Should he choose to stay, he can maintain that special daily relationship, remaining a crucial figure in their lives. If he departs, however, compromises are nearly unavoidable, resulting in pain for him and his offspring. Our society is teeming with men who see their children less than they desire and children who yearn for their father's daily presence.

As his 'third age', a gentle euphemism for growing old, envelopes him, he feels even worse. Now even less esteemed by our society's relentless fixation on youth and productivity, he engages in a futile battle against physical decay. Having defined himself by his work, material success, physical prowess and social status, he is suddenly left without any anchor for his self-esteem. If he is also bereft of any significant relationships—with a partner, children, or family—he is at a heightened risk of feeling alienated from life, with no purpose and even less meaning.

5

Patriarchy: The Four Toxic Values

Let's examine the concept of patriarchy in more detail. Patriarchy has a long and complex history, with roots in ancient civilisations. The social structure typically involves men holding the majority of power in governing roles and in the household, leaving women largely excluded. In ancient Rome, for example, the "pater familias" held legal and moral authority over the family, including his wife, children, and slaves. The Ancient Greeks, following on from the Mesopotamian civilisations, located all power and authority in the male of the family. Women were 'protected' by being sequestered and having no public life outside of religious duties.

As European civilisations developed out of the Roman Empire, they developed Feudal systems that retained the patriarchal systems of male dominance. This not only affected women. Patriarchal systems divide men into classes that are unequally valued. By separating men into different groups with different roles and access to resources, those men who were born into the top class had the opportunity to hoard wealth and, therefore, power. Those men then supported the "patriarch", often called the king, and in return for providing him with the means to rule, they would all consolidate their ongoing accumulation of wealth and power. A perfect example of this is the English Medieval description of society. 'Those who rule, those who pray and those who work'. The vast majority of men were relegated to the third class.

If we look at this through the lens of feminist analysis that critiques male-dominated social structures, what we see is that men were also reduced to their biological functions, their brute strength and their physical labour, just as women were reduced to their sexual and childbearing capacity. Simone de Beauvoir called women the 'Second Sex', excluded from the realm of freedom and transcendence that had been afforded to men. Similarly, Carole Pateman suggested in "The Sexual Contract" that traditional contract theory is, in fact, a patriarchal structure that always benefits men at the expense of women. When we examine these ideas within the construct of class-based systems, what we find is that although all men were held in higher esteem than women, only some men had any actual agency in their own lives.

By examining the ways in which patriarchal structures are embedded in our social and political systems, feminist theories offer valuable insights into the ongoing struggles for sexual and civil equality and justice for both women and men in today's world. From a sociological perspective, patriarchy is a social structure in which men possess the predominant power and influence in areas such as political leadership, moral authority, and property control. Sylvia Walby's "Theorising Patriarchy" provides a comprehensive framework for comprehending the dynamics of patriarchy, including factors such as paid employment, the state's role, male aggression, sexual norms, and the functioning of the household.

Psychological research looks at the effects of patriarchal structures on individuals and groups. This encompasses issues such as gender-role stress and expectations, internalised sexism, and systemic biases. For instance, Janet Shibley Hyde's "The Gender Similarities Hypothesis" examines how patriarchal social structures perpetuate gender stereotypes, thereby contributing to individual and institutional biases. Additionally, psychologists investigate how patriarchal norms affect mental health. Men may experience pressure to conform to patriarchal ideals of masculinity, leading to stress, aggression, or emotional repression. On the other hand, women's response to oppression can include anxiety, body image concerns, and low self-esteem due to patriarchal standards.

These analyses of patriarchy highlight the complex and multifaceted nature of the ideology that is deeply entrenched in all aspects of our society, and the implications are far-reaching. The interconnectedness of how these beliefs shape individuals and the institutions that dominate and control our society impact individual and collective experiences.

But what does Patriarchy look like in action?

The questions I posed at the start of this section are related to the four key characteristics that I argue form the system we call Patriarchy. First, bell hook writes in her article 'Understanding Patriarchy', "that most men do not use the word patriarchy in everyday life. Most men never even think about patriarchy—what it means, how it is created and sustained." And that is at the core of the problem.

Men need to explicitly understand how we have been socialised in patriarchal beliefs and values to know what we are dealing with. I will start with an outline of how a patriarchal construction of the four core values of patriarchy has impacted men and how it has been reflected in our organisations and institutions in a way that has led to numerous serious issues locally and globally. To get a handle on the impact of Patriarchy on men and society in general, we need to consider the implications of the four critical values of patriarchy.

- Territorial
- Hierarchical
- Acquisitional
- Competitive.

How is this ideological? Ideologies are the beliefs, values, and attitudes that shape how we perceive and interact with the world, both at conscious and unconscious levels. They provide a framework for understanding society, determining norms, and guiding actions. One such ideology is patriarchy, which is a system of beliefs that includes the justification and perpetuation of male dominance and female subordination. This ideology influences social norms, values, and practices in ways that privilege some men and disadvantage all women while also shaping our understanding of concepts such as gender. Gender is the name we have given to the traditional beliefs, descriptions, expectations and behaviours that are mandated for each of the sexes. Instead of seeing ourselves as human beings who, as individuals, have our own talents, strengths and interests, we have shaped ourselves into two rigidly defined types of humans.

In summary, Patriarchy operates as an ideology in several key ways. Firstly, it promotes the traits of dominance, competition, and control associated with masculinity as valuable while devaluing traits such as empathy, nurturing, and co-operation, locating them within the construct of femininity. This reinforces gender hierarchies and perpetuates inequality. Secondly, patriarchal ideology prescribes specific roles and expectations for men and women, limiting individual potential and reinforcing inequality. For example, even now, in the twenty-first century, men are often expected to be strong, rational providers. In contrast, women are often expected to be caring, emotional, and focused on family responsibilities. Thirdly, patriarchal beliefs are embedded in social, political, and economic institutions and practices, ranging from laws and policies that disadvantage women to cultural practices that reinforce gender norms that limit acceptable life choices for men.

One of the most insidious aspects of patriarchy is its normalisation. The ideology is often so deeply ingrained in society that it is seen as 'natural' or 'the way things are'. This normalisation makes it difficult to challenge patriarchal beliefs and practices. Finally, patriarchy intersects with other ideologies, such as racism, classism, and heteronormativity, compounding the effects of patriarchal ideology and leading to multiple layers of oppression for certain groups of people.

In its essence patriarchy is an ideology that shapes social norms, values, and practices in ways that privilege men and disadvantage women. It promotes values associated with masculinity while devaluing those traits that are associated with the feminine, prescribes specific roles and expectations for men and women, and is embedded in social, political, and economic institutions and practices. Its normalisation makes it difficult to challenge, and its intersections with other ideologies can compound the effects of patriarchal ideology.

An example of how embedded patriarchy is in most societies can be seen in the levels of inequality that exists in many nations, even modern western democracies. The negative effect of the traditional hierarchical approach to power within patriarchy leads to an uneven distribution of resources and opportunities, which prevents most members of the community from reaching their full potential. Poverty and alienation leads to mental health issues, which are on the rise in many communities across the world. As we noted earlier, four core values are the foundation of patriarchy.

The First Toxic Value: Territoriality.

Territoriality is characterised by the urge to assert control or ownership over a particular resource or area. Territorial behaviour can provide both subtle and obvious benefits to humans. Personalising our homes and workplaces, for example, can create a sense of comfort and well-being, providing a refuge from the chaos of the outside world. Similarly, our social relationships are marked by certain territorial boundaries, albeit more emotional and intellectual than physical.

Nature documentaries like David Attenborough's Breathtaking Chronicles, show us the ubiquitous nature of territoriality among all manner of creatures, whether avian, reptilian, insect, or mammalian. Much of their time and energy is invested in acquiring, delineating, and defending territories; a ceaseless struggle punctuated only by the primal call to procreate. Indeed, the stakes are often as stark for them as life and death.

It's a potent reminder that the impetus to mark territory is not an arbitrary construct but an integral facet of existence across most species.

It is a common belief that, being animals, humans naturally gravitate toward territorial behaviour. However, this is not entirely accurate. Over the course of centuries, humans have tended to migrate and explore, which is a defining feature of our species. While our closest genetic relatives, primates, do exhibit territorial behaviour, this trait is not necessarily relevant to humans. Our evolution as a species has brought about fundamental changes in our neural pathways since the dawn of our consciousness and sentience. Contrary to popular belief, humans are not genetically predisposed to territoriality. Socialised values, including characteristics of patriarchy, have been integrated into a framework that results in an ideology, taught to us through our cultures.

Humans are distinguished from other animals by our innate curiosity, which propels us to explore and conquer new territories. When we discover uncharted areas, we stake our claim on them. However, the act of claiming ownership is not instinctual but rather a conscious and deliberate practice.

As a species, we have flourished and reproduced, driven by our desire to access resources and expand our reach. Our curiosity has now taken us beyond the confines of Earth to explore the distant corners of our solar system. This expansion manifests our nomadic curiosity rather than an inherent territorial impulse.

Defining the Human Concept of Territory:

Within patriarchal societies, the concept of territoriality extends beyond physical spaces to encompass social, economic, and political spheres. This characteristic is heavily intertwined with power dynamics and the control exerted by men over various aspects of life. Traditionally, men have controlled and dominated numerous physical spaces such as workplaces, government, and public arenas. Women's entry into these spaces was, and in some cases still is, seen as an invasion of 'male territory'. This can result in significant resistance and sexism towards women entering the workforce or politics. Being territorial can mean defining and controlling cultural norms, social roles, and family structures in social contexts.

Traditionally men have asserted their dominance in patriarchal societies by dictating cultural and social norms. This has manifested historically, and in some current societies in gender segregation, with men and women having distinctly different roles and spaces. This perpetuates stereotypes and hinders mutual understanding and respect. In extreme cases, asserting male dominance over certain territories can result in oppression and violence against women. This can range from domestic abuse to social practices that control and limit women's freedom and safety in social spaces and can involve shaming or ostracising women who don't conform to traditional gender roles. The economic disparity between men and women has been a long-standing consequence of the separation of life into male and female realms.

The assertion of 'male territory' led to environments that are hostile to women, one of which is the workplace. Men have traditionally had access to resources and held the majority of society's wealth and property, leaving women with limited economic opportunities. Even in modern societies where women now have the right to own property and earn income, they often face systemic barriers that hinder their full economic participation. In workplaces, traditionally the territory of men, women can face sexist discrimination, sexual harassment, and entrenched systems that devalue their success. One of the most prominent examples of this is the 'wage gap', which refers to the phenomenon of women being paid less than their male counterparts for performing the same job. This disparity has no justification, is unethical and is found across many industries. It is an artefact of the devaluing of women as workers and the entrenched and often unconscious belief in men's superiority.

The problems stemming from patriarchal territoriality are manifold because the idea that men should be dominant and territorial not only harms women, it reinforces toxic masculinity among men. Toxic masculinity includes behaviours and attitudes, such as aggression, violence, and the suppression of emotions. Not all men are comfortable being dominant or territorial, but social expectations can make them feel like they must act against their nature. This can cause stress and internal conflict as they struggle to fit into a narrow definition of masculinity.

The concept of territoriality is much more influential than most of us realise. Emotional territoriality is rarely recognised, let alone discussed. A common example of the reach of territoriality is in the expectation that men should not openly express emotions such as sadness or vulnerability, as it is seen as a sign of weakness and goes against the social expectation of masculinity. On the other hand, women are expected to be comfortable being emotional and nurturing. However, they are also expected to control and suppress certain emotions, such as anger or assertiveness, as these are viewed as too masculine or threatening. These gendered expectations of emotional expression have carved up normal human emotion into particular territories that are then located within the biological understanding of each sex. Men are seen to be 'biologically' incapable of being nurturing, and women are seen as biologically determined to be nurturing. This can and does lead to individuals of both sexes feeling like they need to conform to prescribed emotional norms in order to fit in and be accepted by society, which can be damaging to their mental health and well-being.

The assignment of different emotional states to the two sexes not only artificially divides normal human emotional states into a sexist paradigm, but it also accords positive and negative valuing systems to these emotions. In patriarchal ideology, men are typically expected to be emotionally controlled, exhibiting control, stoicism, and rationality. This is valued as a positive trait of men and means that they are capable of being the decision-makers in society. Expressing emotions, particularly those associated with vulnerability such as fear, sadness, or even joy, can be perceived as a sign of weakness and a breach of the 'male emotional territory'. This can lead to men suppressing their emotions or expressing them through socially 'acceptable' outlets, often aggression or withdrawal.

Conversely, women are assigned the emotional territory of empathy, sensitivity, and care. They are expected to be emotionally expressive and have been assigned the role of emotional caretakers. However, this emotional expressivity is devalued, controlled and policed, with 'women's' emotions and their expression dismissed as irrational or overblown, particularly in public or professional settings. These beliefs not only reinforce harmful stereotypes that dictate our self-perceptions but also what we expect from others around us, which interferes with communication in all of our relationships. Emotional territoriality is a big part of how men and women misunderstand and hurt each other in relationships, which can lead to social and emotional isolation. When individuals exhibit excessive territorial behaviour in any sphere of their lives, they may isolate themselves from collaborative efforts; in any sphere of their lives, they may isolate themselves from collaborative efforts or prevent meaningful connections with others.

The Second Toxic Value: Hierarchy.

Patriarchal systems are characterised by establishing hierarchical structures favouring some men over other men and all women. These structures perpetuate the idea that some individuals have more worth and are inherently superior to everyone else. Added to territoriality, this ensures that those at the top of the hierarchy not only have power, they also have control of the resources. Historically, within the patriarchal paradigm, sustaining this power has required a culture of dominance and submission, leading to the abuse of power and the disregard for the rights and viewpoints of those occupying lower positions in society. This has had far-reaching consequences, including perpetuating sex-based, racist and classicist discrimination and marginalising those who do not conform to traditional roles.

In modern democracies today, the concept of hierarchy remains entrenched and continues to influence every facet of the way our societies function. It is manifest in the larger picture of our political, corporate and class-based systems. It is the reason why, despite the legal and social changes that have enabled women to access the public world, men continue to hold primary power and authority in society.

In social structures among men, hierarchy is a common feature that determines the perceived levels of authority, influence, or power of individuals or groups. This hierarchy often emerges from competition for status, dominance, and resources. Men may try to establish their positions in these hierarchies through different means, including displays of strength, charisma, or control. Hierarchy reinforces these competitive behaviours, along with physical displays of power, verbal assertiveness or aggression and emotional suppression.

Men often actively vie for positions of influence within social groups, workplaces, and even family structures which interferes with the cohesiveness of the group and can lead to exclusion and the formation of cliques and a concentration of power within the select few, which is a core feature of hierarchies. This contributes to toxic behaviours that lead to strained relationships that can result in resentment, conflict and the destruction of genuine connections.

While hierarchy may appear to be a natural aspect of human social dynamics, it isn't. What is important is to recognise the negative impact it has on men's well-being and their relationships. One of the most significant issues is the toll it can take on men's mental health. The constant pressure to establish dominance and maintain one's position in the hierarchy can lead to stress, anxiety, and depression. Men might feel compelled to conceal their vulnerabilities to maintain their status, resulting in further emotional strain. Additionally, a rigid hierarchy can limit opportunities for personal growth and development, discouraging men from pursuing interests or roles outside their designated status, leading to a lack of fulfilment and a sense of stagnancy.

Consider a scenario where a group of male friends regularly spends time together. One of the men consistently seeks to establish his dominance by diminishing the accomplishments of his peers and dominating conversations. Although this individual may feel a temporary sense of superiority, his actions ultimately serve to alienate his friends, eroding trust and camaraderie within the group.

Now imagine a workplace where a male employee persistently undermines his colleagues in an attempt to curry favour with the higher-ups. As he climbs the corporate ladder, his actions create a toxic work environment, leading to decreased morale and productivity among his colleagues.

In both of these scenarios, the negative impact of hierarchical behaviours on men's well-being and relationships is clearly evident. It is crucial to recognise the pitfalls of such behaviours and to cultivate environments that prioritise collaboration, empathy, and mutual respect. Ultimately, these efforts can lead to healthier social structures and stronger relationships among men.

This hierarchy can be difficult to dismantle, but it is essential for the well-being of all of us to create a more just and equitable society in which everyone, men, women and minority groups, have equal representation in decision-making processes. Patriarchy's strict hierarchical structure enforces rigid gender roles and class structures, undermines cooperation and leads to conflict.

The Third Toxic Value: Acquisition.

The act of striving to gather resources and influence is known as being acquisitional. Throughout history, patriarchal societies, which have been the predominant type of society, have operated by giving power and authority over resources to select men. As a result, those men at the top of the hierarchy have accumulated a disproportionate amount of wealth, property, and opportunities in comparison to other men and women. From a viewpoint of fair distribution, the more patriarchal a society is, the greater the inequality that exists within it. This inequality allows a small group of people to dominate those lower in the hierarchy by restricting their access to necessary resources, thus preventing them from improving their own life circumstances.

This also leads men to pursue and accumulate material possessions, status symbols, prestige and achievements as a means of establishing their worth and dominance within society. This behaviour stems from patriarchal stereotypical expectations that equate success and masculinity with the possession of wealth, power, and external markers of achievement. This means that when acquisition is added to the hierarchy, the drive to sequester power and resources into as few hands as possible is enhanced.

The acquisition-focused behaviours among men can manifest in various ways. One common expression is the acquisition of material possessions such as luxury items, expensive cars, and gadgets, which are often regarded as symbols of social status and success. Another manifestation is the pursuit of high-paying careers and positions of authority, which can be driven by a desire to accumulate wealth and assert dominance. Men may also engage in competitive behaviours to achieve higher ranks, awards, or accolades, thereby showcasing their superiority. These are merely a few instances of how acquisition-focused behaviours can manifest among men.

While the pursuit of success and acquisition can be a powerful motivator, it's important to consider the potential negative impacts that can arise from an excessive focus on obtaining material possessions. One significant drawback is the risk of becoming overly materialistic, where a person's sense of self-worth becomes tied to what they own rather than who they are as an individual. This can lead to a superficial and unsatisfying existence, as the pursuit of external markers of success fails to bring lasting happiness.

In contemporary society, a considerable number of individuals possess a strong desire to amass large amounts of material possessions and exhibit their worth, leading to a culture of competition rather than collaboration. This mindset, not only devalues non material aspects of life, it unfortunately discourages individuals from expressing their emotions and vulnerability, as these traits are perceived as a disadvantage in a competitive environment. Consequently, relationships become superficial, and people prioritise their personal achievements over meaningful connections with others. This social pressure has been linked to various mental health problems, including stress, anxiety, and depression.

It's important to take a step back and consider the negative impact of our pursuit of material success and acquisition, and focus more on ensuring that we prioritise our emotional and mental well-being, and cultivate genuine relationships with those around us.

Consider a hypothetical situation where a male individual relentlessly pursues career advancements and job titles, putting in long hours at the expense of his own physical and emotional health as well as his interpersonal relationships. Despite achieving success in the eyes of society, he continues to struggle with burnout and strained personal connections. The detrimental impact of a mindset that solely focuses on acquiring external markers of success, such as wealth and status, on men's overall life satisfaction, interpersonal relationships, and emotional well-being should not be underestimated. It's crucial for men to strike a balance between personal growth and the pursuit of such markers and to shift towards values that prioritise genuine connections, emotional well-being, and holistic fulfilment.

The Fourth Toxic Value: Competition.

Competition is an integral part of human nature that can have both positive or negative effects. Patriarchal ideology uses competition to divide people by pitting them against each other and promoting dominance which aligns with the other three values of patriarchy. Competing to be at the top of the hierarchy, to control more territory and to acquire more wealth or power. In the context of competition among men it involves striving for superiority and recognition, and it equates success and masculinity with outperforming others. In fact, the competitive ethos devalues traits such as empathy, cooperation, and nurturing, all of which are vital for building strong, supportive relationships and communities.

Another outlet for male competitiveness is through athletic pursuits. Sports and physical activities can become arenas for showcasing dominance and outperforming competitors. This can range from casual sports and games with friends, to professional-level competition. Although competition is an essential aspect of the world of sport, if winning is the only measure of success and is prioritised over teamwork, cooperation, and empathy, it can lead to negative outcomes. For instance, some athletes may resort to cheating or using performance-enhancing drugs to win, which not only harms their opponents but also discredits the integrity of the sport. Cooperation, empathy and teamwork encourage collaboration and recognise the unique strengths and talents of all of those involved, providing a space for both competition and a respectful attitude.

While competition can be a driving force behind personal growth and innovation, it's important to acknowledge the potential negative impacts of an excessive focus on competition. One of the most significant drawbacks is the erosion of relationships, as individuals may prioritise their personal gain over genuine connections and cooperation. Mental health struggles can also arise from the pressure to constantly outperform and prove oneself. In an unhealthy competitive environment, toxic aspects of traditional masculinity can be reinforced, such as suppressing emotions and prioritising dominance. Furthermore, intense competition can exacerbate inequalities and exclude those who don't conform to the dominant competitive norms. Lastly, overemphasis on competition might discourage collaboration, hindering the sharing of ideas, innovations, and mutual support. It's crucial to strike a balance between healthy competition and collaboration to avoid these negative consequences

Imagine a social setting where a man is always trying to outdo his friends in every conversation, often belittling their opinions. This type of behaviour creates a sense of alienation and tension within the group, ultimately weakening the bonds of friendship. It's evident that this excessive competitiveness has a negative impact on men's well-being, relationships, and overall sense of community. It's important to promote healthy competition that encourages personal growth and development while still fostering empathy, cooperation, and genuine connections.

The Fifth Toxic Value: Combativeness.

This refers to the tendency of men to engage in confrontational and aggressive behaviours within social contexts. This behaviour often arises from social expectations that valorise dominance, strength, and assertiveness as markers of masculinity. Within male social structures, combativeness can manifest as a desire to establish authority, win arguments, and project an image of power. When it comes to combative behaviours among men, there are various ways in which it can manifest. One common form is through verbal confrontations, where men may use aggressive language and engage in arguments to assert their dominance and win debates. Another way is through physical displays, where in certain situations, men may resort to posturing and confrontations to establish their dominance. However, combativeness can also lead to an egocentric focus, where individuals prioritise their own interests over cooperation and collaboration. It's important to recognise these behaviours and find ways to address them in a peaceful and respectful manner.

While it's important to stand up for oneself, an excessive focus on combativeness can have negative consequences. Firstly, it can strain relationships, causing conflicts, misunderstandings, and a lack of genuine connections. Additionally, it can reinforce aspects of toxic masculinity, such as suppressing emotions and glorifying aggression. The constant need to assert dominance and engage in confrontations can also lead to chronic stress and mental health struggles. Overly combative behaviour inhibits open communication and hinders the exchange of ideas and perspectives. Finally, combativeness can discourage vulnerability, as individuals fear that showing vulnerability might be perceived as weakness.

Consider a social situation where a man persistently interjects and monopolises discussions, rendering it difficult for others to articulate their views. His confrontational conduct obstructs meaningful dialogue and discourages open exchange, which spoils everyone's enjoyment of the gathering.

In a professional environment, envision a male colleague

who consistently undermines his team members during meetings, aiming to establish himself as the dominant decision-maker. His confrontational demeanour stifles teamwork and impedes the team's potential.

In both instances, the detrimental effects of an excessive focus on combativeness on men's well-being, relationships, and overall sense of community become apparent. It is vital to promote assertiveness in a constructive and considerate manner, prioritising empathy, cooperation, and efficient communication.

6

The Psychological Consequences of Patriarchal Values: - Normative Male Alexithymia, Reduced Empathy, Acquired Narcissism, and Psychopathy:

The impacts of patriarchy as a social system are pervasive, informing social norms, individual behaviours, and the nuances of interpersonal dynamics. This chapter delves into the disturbing psychological fallouts of patriarchy—specifically, reduced empathy, acquired narcissism, and psychopathy—and how the values of territoriality, hierarchy, acquisition, and competition fuel these traits.

Normative Male Alexithymia:

One of the key issues affecting men psychologically is what psychiatry has dubbed *Normative Male Alexithymia*. It is a term used to describe a phenomenon where men, influenced by traditional masculine norms, struggle to identify, express, or communicate their emotional experiences. This personality construct, characterised by an inability to identify and describe one's feelings, isn't limited to males. However, the term "normative male alexithymia" is used to discuss how social norms and expectations exacerbate or encourage alexithymic traits, specifically among men.

In patriarchal cultures, men are socialised to suppress emotions perceived as "weak" or "feminine," like vulnerability, sadness, or fear. However, other emotions such as compassion, nurturing and tolerance are also included among the feminine emotional states. Men are encouraged to express "masculine" emotions like anger or pride and to solve problems through action rather than through emotional introspection or dialogue. This socialisation can contribute to a kind of emotional illiteracy.

The implications of normative male Alexithymia are vast and far-reaching. Difficulty in identifying and expressing emotions can lead to problems in relationships, including difficulties in marital and familial relationships. Furthermore, an inability to understand or express emotion contributes to increased stress, undiagnosed mental health issues, and poor coping strategies, such as substance abuse. Additionally, emotional suppression has been linked to a range of physical health problems, including cardiovascular issues and decreased immune function.

Acquired Narcissism:

Acquired narcissism, characterised by grandiosity, a profound need for admiration, and a notable lack of empathy (American Psychiatric Association, 2013), is often incited by the patriarchal values of territoriality, hierarchy, acquisition and competition.

Territorial behaviours, such as asserting control over intellectual spaces, tend to inflate self-worth and propagate narcissistic traits. Hierarchical structures further reinforce this inflated self-perception, allowing those in power to develop a sense of superiority and entitlement. The value of acquisition—the desire to amass power and resources—is also congruent with narcissistic tendencies for personal gain and prestige. For instance, wealth disparities between men and also between men and women, even in developed societies, demonstrate how acquisition often fuels a sense of superiority in men, leading to acquired narcissism (Sen, 1990).

Reduced Empathy

Empathy, the ability to resonate with the feelings and experiences of others, faces significant attrition in patriarchal systems. This is primarily the result of the values of territoriality and hierarchy. Territoriality promotes an 'us versus them' mindset. A salient example is seen in the world of technology, where it is predominantly male-dominated and women often feel excluded. This sense of exclusivity and ownership fuels a lack of empathy for 'outsiders', potentially breeding toxic and discriminatory environments (Brown, 2009).

Hierarchical structures prevalent in patriarchal societies exacerbate this lack of empathy. For instance, men are overwhelmingly represented in leadership positions in the corporate world. The power dynamics of this structure can instil a sense of entitlement in those at the top, diminishing their motivation to empathise with those lower in the hierarchy (Connell, 2005).

Psychopathy

Psychopathy is marked by persistent antisocial behaviour, diminished empathy, boldness, and egotistical traits (Hare & Neumann, 2008), which can find a fertile breeding ground in patriarchal societies. The value of competition, a cornerstone of patriarchal societies, often begets these psychopathic tendencies. Contact sports like football offer a microcosm of this competitive drive. However, the corporate world, where aggression is often praised and empathy dismissed in the competitive climb to the top, is the modern realm of psychopathy. Constant competition can trigger a lack of empathy, heightened aggression, and in extreme cases, psychopathic tendencies (Kimmel, 2008).

The patriarchal value of hierarchy also significantly encourages psychopathic traits by endorsing a culture of dominance and subordination, potentially leading to callousness and manipulativeness.

Implications and Consequences:

The psychological ramifications of reduced empathy, acquired narcissism, and psychopathy have serious social and interpersonal repercussions. On a personal individual level, they lead to impaired relationships and diminished psychological well-being, with increased interpersonal violence, which then leads to significant social disruption (Ronningstam, 2016).

Hence, understanding the roots of these negative psychological traits in patriarchal values underscores the urgency of social and individual efforts to challenge these values. The goal must be to nurture a more empathetic, equitable society where destructive psychological traits are curbed, not cultivated. We need to challenge the belief that reason and emotion are oppositional traits, and that we as individuals, cannot be both reasonable and in touch with our emotions. The 'either /or' proposition that is entrenched in patriarchal ideology is based on a belief in biological determinism that has underpinned the allocation of half of our normal human functioning to each of the two sexes. The characteristics and capacities attributed to men and women are what we call 'gender' stereotypes. Men are described as being biologically driven by reason and incapable of expressing emotions, while women are believed to be driven by emotions and incapable of rationality.

We know this is not true. The human experience is a complex tapestry woven from various threads, including physical, intellectual, and emotional components. Because it had been traditionally devalued, the emotional realm often proves elusive and misunderstood, yet to deny the power and influence of our emotions is to deny a fundamental aspect of our humanity. Men have been socialised to suppress or repress their emotions, leading to a profound disconnect from their inner selves and a lack of intimacy in their interpersonal relationships. This makes the emotional realm a place of great uncertainty and danger, where our deepest fears and anxieties reside. Unfortunately, many of us are reluctant to venture into this realm, fearing exposure and vulnerability. Despite this resistance, we must embrace the full range of our emotions. Doing so can unlock the potential for deep emotional connection and well-being. The act of embracing our emotions in their entirety, both light and dark, allows us to experience the richness of life fully.

Encouraging emotional intelligence in men, particularly

within a patriarchal society, requires a concerted effort to challenge and uproot long-standing social norms and stereotypes related to masculinity. This is no small feat, and it demands the implementation of a range of effective strategies that can help foster a more nuanced and inclusive understanding of what it means to be a man. Whether through targeted educational initiatives, community outreach programs, or other forms of intervention, it is essential that we work together to create a culture that values emotional intelligence and recognises its importance in shaping healthy relationships, strong communities, and a more just and equitable society for all.

One of the most effective ways to promote emotional literacy is to teach it, both in the home and at school. All children, boys and girls, need to have their emotional reactions explained and named. Parent's and extended family should all be involved in normalising children's experiences of feeling emotions and expressing them in appropriate ways from an early age. They should be taught that all emotions, including those typically associated with vulnerability, such as sadness or fear, are normal and healthy parts of the human experience. That having an emotion is a cue to thinking about what is happening to you or to those around you. It is important to teach children that feeling, for example the emotion of anger, does not mean they should act in an angry, and possibly aggressive manner. Emotions should lead to understanding, and an increase in self awareness and good choices about how to respond to what caused the emotion in the first place..

Having an emotionally intelligent male role model in one's life can significantly impact how one perceives and expresses emotions. Fathers, for example, can show their sons that crying, feeling vulnerable, and expressing emotions healthily is acceptable. This can counter the patriarchal influence that associates masculinity with emotional repression and stoicism and demonstrate that masculinity and emotional expression are not mutually exclusive. The more men who reject the traditional attitude to expressing their emotions, the more normal and acceptable it becomes to do so.

Similarly, teachers can play an essential role in promoting emotional intelligence among boys. They can help boys understand and manage their emotions by creating a safe and supportive classroom environment where they can express themselves. For instance, a teacher may encourage a boy who is feeling frustrated to talk about his emotions instead of suppressing them, thus helping the boy develop a healthy relationship with his emotions and express them in a way that does not harm himself or others. Promoting emotional intelligence in education is also crucial. School curricula could include emotional intelligence as a key competency and teaching skills like emotional regulation, empathy, and interpersonal communication from an early age.

Moreover, sports coaches can be positive male role models promoting healthy emotional expression. They can teach boys that it's okay to show their emotions on the field, whether it's enthusiasm, frustration, or disappointment. For example, a coach may praise a player for showing passion and intensity during a game, even if it involves tears or raised voices. This can help boys understand that expressing their emotions appropriately is a sign of strength, not weakness.

It is imperative to have male role models to actively promote healthy emotional expression and dismantle toxic stereotypes surrounding masculinity. They must demonstrate that expressing a full range of emotions is acceptable and does not diminish one's masculinity. This will positively impact boys' mental health and well-being and, ultimately, the entire society.

Acquiring emotional regulation is another crucial skill that everyone must master. It is essential to manage emotions in a healthy manner to prevent being overwhelmed or reacting negatively. For instance, in stressful situations, emotional regulation enables individuals to maintain composure and refrain from overreacting. This is where being able to recognise and label your emotions is integral to being able to regulate your expression of your feelings. Additionally, mindfulness can be a powerful tool in the practice of emotional regulation. This involves being fully present in the moment and non-judgmentally focusing on your thoughts and emotions. Through this practice, you can develop a heightened self-awareness and gain greater control over your emotional responses.

It is worth noting that emotional regulation is an ongoing process that requires persistence and patience. However, consistent effort can lead to increased emotional intelligence, stronger relationships, and a more fulfilling life experience.

Developing empathy is essential to emotional intelligence, particularly for boys and men. By cultivating empathy, they can understand and appreciate the emotions and perspectives of others, which leads to better relationships and communication. One effective way to foster empathy is through activities such as reading books or articles that feature diverse characters and experiences. Literature has always been a teaching resource for understanding ourselves and others through the medium of a story with its resolution of human dilemmas and conflicts. Encouraging individuals to step into someone else's shoes and see the world from their perspective can help build empathy and create a more compassionate society.

Creating safe spaces for emotional expression is also essential. Boys and men need environments where they feel safe to express their emotions without judgment or ridicule. This could be within the family, at school, in therapy, or in support groups.

Challenging harmful stereotypes about emotional expression is another important strategy. Encouraging critical thinking about gender norms and stereotypes can help boys and men question and challenge the often narrow depictions of masculinity presented in movies, TV shows, and video games. Encouraging positive masculinity that celebrates emotional openness, respect for others, empathy, and care can also help promote emotional intelligence in men.

Additionally, normalising help-seeking for emotional struggles and combatting the stigma around it is essential. Men should be encouraged to seek support when needed, whether from trusted friends and family, support groups, or mental health professionals.

By employing these strategies, we can work towards a society where emotional intelligence is valued and nurtured in both men and women. This can lead to healthier, happier individuals and more equitable relationships and communities.

One of the most well-known consequences of emotional illiteracy is that men have historically struggled with emotional expression, particularly regarding communication and conflict resolution. This struggle has far-reaching consequences, affecting not only their relationships with their partners and children but also their friendships and professional relationships. One of the most common complaints from women in relationships is that their male partners don't communicate effectively. This lack of communication leads to confusion, misunderstandings and conflict. In fact, studies have shown that men who struggle with emotional expression are more likely to engage in aggressive behaviour, both in their personal relationships and in other areas of their lives.

So why do men struggle with communication? Part of the problem is that we have been socialised to prioritise rationality over emotion. The cultural conditioning of men to hide their feelings can make it difficult for them to open up and share their thoughts and feelings with others. However, the consequences of this lack of emotional expression are significant in both personal and professional relationships. Poor communication leads to misunderstandings, resentment, and the eventual breakdown of the relationship itself. In the workplace, it can lead to ineffective collaboration, missed opportunities, and a toxic work environment (2).

The good news is that emotional intelligence can be learned and developed at any age. By practising mindfulness, empathy, and active listening, men can learn to understand their own emotions better and communicate them effectively to others. This can lead to more harmonious relationships, improved work performance, and a more fulfilling life.

The Problem with Conflict:

Some men may find conflict resolution challenging, as they have often been taught to behave aggressively in specific settings like sports or work. They have also sometimes been raised in households where they were exposed to unhealthy approaches to conflict. Let's be clear. Aggression is never an appropriate way to manage conflict, and it is not effective as it creates more problems, which often end up with worse consequences.

When it comes to personal relationships, aggression is not only inappropriate and an ineffective way to resolve conflicts, it can destroy the relationship and even lead to violence. Because of this, some men choose to avoid conflict to maintain peace, even if it means compromising their own desires and needs. This can cause them and their partners to feel frustrated and resentful and thus also end up ruining the relationship.

When approaching conflict in personal relationships, it's important to understand that it's not about winning or losing. It's about finding a solution that works for all those involved, whether they are your partner, a family member or a friend. This requires a collaborative mindset, where both parties are willing to listen to each other's perspectives and work together to find a resolution. One effective strategy for resolving conflicts is active listening. This means fully engaging with the other person's point of view and trying to understand their perspective. Doing so lets you identify the underlying issues and concerns driving the conflict and work towards a mutually beneficial solution. This requires communication.

An important aspect of effective conflict resolution is being able to express your own needs and desires clearly and respectfully while also being open to the other person's needs and desires. This can involve compromise and negotiation in order to find a solution that works for all involved. By approaching conflict collaboratively and respectfully, men can build stronger, more resilient relationships with their partners, friends, family and colleagues. Conflict can be an opportunity for growth and deeper understanding rather than a source of tension and stress. Emotional intelligence is a crucial skill for both men and women to develop in order to build healthy, fulfilling relationships and succeed in all areas of life. By learning to communicate effectively and resolve conflicts constructively and collaboratively, we can all build stronger, more resilient relationships and create a more fulfilling life for ourselves and those around us.

A fundamental aspect of the way conflict impacts our relationships is that it is often driven by an unconscious and deeply ingrained concept of territory. Traditional patriarchal human socialisation teaches us to set up boundaries around ourselves and also around the other people in our lives.

The Consequences of Patriarchy on The Institutions in Society.

It is common for contemporary Western establishments and institutions to employ the conventional patriarchal model, which marginalises women, consequently maintaining a male-dominated domain. Understandably, women were not initially considered when most of our public culture was established. Throughout the existence of current nation-states and the accompanying development of cultural, educational, and commercial institutions, women were effectively excluded from public life. The implementation of a dualistic separation of human activity into public and private spheres placed all areas of the economy, politics, education, and decision-making in the public sphere, which was the responsibility of men. Women were relegated to the private, inner sphere of home and family.

This division was based on perceived biological competencies, subsequently defined as gender differences.

However, many men have also been left out and pushed aside by the cultures of our institutions that favour particular types of men. Women used this exclusion in their arguments for all adults to be considered equal citizens of society. An example of this is the right to vote. Initially, in the British Empire and the USA, only white men who owned property were given the right to vote. By arguing for the enfranchisement of those men who were excluded, based on their personhood as defined within liberal democratic thinking, women were then able to demonstrate that they also fulfilled this requirement of personhood and should also have the right to vote.

Having argued that women were the same sort of human person as men, they had highlighted their capacity to act in accordance with the values and behaviours that remained valued by patriarchal ideology. This meant that as they entered the world of work, they were expected to conform to the system as it was. To align themselves with patriarchal ideals and attitudes. Not doing so meant that they would not be accepted and could not succeed. The power suit, with its massive shoulder pads, which were the uniform of corporate women in the 1980s, was a way of signalling women's compliance with the status quo.

Upon initial examination, it appeared that reason had emerged victorious. The arguments put forth by women and their supporters were grounded in logic and reason. Evidently, there was no rationale for one half of the population to dominate the other. Women had demonstrated their competence, proving themselves to be just as capable as men. We as a society have achieved equality. Or had we?

Apart from the well-documented ongoing issues of the vast difference between the legal and social acceptance of equality and the enactment of it within the actual institutions, there was another significant problem that remains entrenched in society. Our valuing system remains patriarchal.

Women succeed by acting like men. Unfortunately, men have often taken over the conversation about equality and twisted it to mean sameness. This misguided approach led to the idea of homogeneity being embraced, with some suggesting that androgyny is the answer to women being accepted into positions of power. The concept of equality as sameness not only diminishes the wonderful diversity of humans and their ways of being in the world, it is morally and literally flawed. The concept of equality of persons is about their having equal worth as humans irrespective of sex, age, colour, or any other difference. The fact that we have yet to truly challenge the ideas that divide us, is evidence of the power of patriarchal ideals.

Having argued for women's equality based on being rational and just like men, we failed to look closely at the sphere from which women had emerged. The private sphere of the home, family, and social and emotional connection remains de valued. We have failed to recognise that all humans are both rational and emotional, and that the interplay of these characteristics is what makes us successful as a species, and as individuals. This is why our institutions remain steeped in an inherently masculine corporate culture that is resisting change. An example of this is the way in which men who want to take paternity leave are often treated with suspicion because they are not prioritising their work over their family.

Another example of the power of patriarchal ideology in the business world is that even now in the twenty-first century, most coaching and mentoring programs in the business world aim to instruct women on how to adopt and utilise masculine traits and behaviours. This emphasis on conformity and uniformity is a defining aspect of the 'territory' or 'domain'. If you want to be a part of men's business, you must pretend to be like a man. And even if you are a man, you still need to conform to the prevailing culture in order to navigate the system and achieve success. What this does, in reality, is limit the diversity of ideas and perspectives in the territory of business, thus continuing to maintain unfair traditional patriarchal ideas about the workplace.

This has also led to an interesting phenomenon: hyper-masculinity. Many men consciously or subconsciously feel the need to increase their masculinity to differentiate themselves from women. This is often reflected in their interest in sports, fitness, and appearance, such as the trend of sporting beards or tattoos. However, not all men feel comfortable being defined by narrow ideas of manhood. Patriarchal institutions are not only alienating and hostile to women, but the many men who do not identify with hyper-masculinity. These men are often subjected to discrimination and disparagement for not fitting into traditional masculine norms..

When we examine masculinity from a critical perspective, it becomes clear that it is a learned behaviour. Regardless of whether or not you fit the stereotypical definition of a patriarchal male, your idea of what it means to be a man has been shaped by the socialisation you have received throughout your life. This is a reality that holds true across all cultures, and our current understanding of the power of this socialisation is backed up by scientific research and psychological studies.

The issue with patriarchal masculinity is that it has been

deeply ingrained into our social structures over thousands of years. This has made it difficult for people to break free from the expectations of being a man in a patriarchal society. As a result, it is often difficult for men to express themselves in ways that do not conform to patriarchal norms. This can cause many problems, including mental health issues, relationship difficulties, and a general sense of dissatisfaction with one's life.

When examining the impact of patriarchy, it is important to consider the role of religion, particularly major global religions like Judaism, Christianity and Islam. These religions reflect institutionalised patriarchal ideologies that have become more traditional and fundamentalist in recent years, according to Giddens (2018). Male-centric theology has been deeply ingrained in these religions, with their theology focused on a male God, resulting in men being viewed as dominant due to their sex, as stated by Klein (2018). This theology quickly gained support from warriors, chieftains, and kings who saw the benefits of aligning themselves with a belief system that reinforced their position in the hierarchy, leading to the accumulation of social power, as also noted by Klein (2018).

To truly understand the impact of patriarchal masculinity, it is important to look at the ways in which it has been institutionalised in our societies. From how we raise boys to the expectations we place on men in the workplace, patriarchal norms are present at every level of our social structure. This can make it difficult for men to break free from these expectations, even if they are aware of the negative impact that they can have on their lives.

Let me illustrate that with some simple examples:

Sport.

When examining the subject of men and their pursuit of sports, it becomes clear that hyper-masculinity plays a significant role. The sports traditionally associated with masculinity often involve aggressive physicality and a focus on domination over opponents. Male teams in these sports dominate the field and hold significant influence in social, commercial, and economic spheres. The social, economic, and commercial value placed on male sports is often greater than on women's sports, perpetuating the notion that hyper-masculine traits are more valuable than other qualities. This emphasis on hyper-masculinity in sports has historically excluded women from participating and continues to present challenges for women seeking funding and resources for their own sports.

My interest is whether this emphasis on male sports actually serves men well. Does it, over our lifetimes, make us more emotionally and behaviourally flexible, and, most importantly, does it make us more resilient? Brooke de Lench, the Founding Executive Director of MomsTeam Institute and the publisher of MomsTeam.com, offers a totally positive overview of sports, boys and men. This is an opinion that is generally held by many people across our culture.

Let me propose some alternative perspectives that challenge de Lench's widely accepted claims regarding sport and boys.

Firstly, *sports are an excellent way for boys to stay active and physically fit, providing them with a healthy outlet to channel their intense physicality and aggression while feeling strong.* This belief that all boys are physically orientated and aggressive is not only accepted as fact, it is seen as a positive. It's probable that some of what de Lench attributes to these activities is accurate to some extent. Sports do make boys fitter, but only in the context where they follow an appropriately supervised programme, wherein we can monitor their physical and emotional stress levels; that is where they are not overtraining. All too often, I and other therapists deal with boys in their teens who are overtrained, fatigued and anxious about their performance.

Secondly, de Lench argues that *not only do sports help boys develop self-control and self-confidence, but they also offer an opportunity to form friendships with other boys.* In fact, in this way of thinking, sports are integral to boys' social relationships, helping them develop skills needed to form competitive groups or coalitions in adulthood, such as in business organisations.

It is also true that these developmental activities also provide practice for specific behavioural skills associated with primitive warfare, such as throwing and tracking the trajectory of projectiles, which historically motivated the creation of some sports. It is why fathers often spend time teaching their sons these skills. Thus, the entrenchment of patriarchal values in warfare is reflected in a lot of the team sports our children play. But there are many other activities that provide the opportunity for boys to make friends and connections and to learn self control and confidence. Sport is just one activity that focuses on group participation.

Thirdly, it is widely believed that *participating in sports can increase a boy's social status, as research shows that male athletes across all sports are significantly more popular than non-athletic male peers.* However, when it comes to self-confidence, friendships, and social status, we must be cautious not to mistake it for narcissism. It is crucial to differentiate between a confident boy and one who only seems confident but relies on his popularity and position on the team to boost his self-esteem. The latter is known as acquired narcissism, which can lead to emotional stress, distress, and susceptibility to follow group norms that are not suitable. Hazing is an example of this phenomenon.

In addition, it is believed that boys who play sports are less likely to smoke cigarettes, use drugs, or consider suicide, making it an effective preventative measure against these behaviours. Another belief is that student-athletes are absent from school 50% less than their peers who do not play sports. However, this reliance on only one aspect of their development means that if something goes wrong, an injury perhaps, and they can no longer participate in the sport that they love, these boys become a very high risk for all those self-destructive behaviours.

Fourthly, participation in sports has also been linked to academic success, as boys who play sports in high school are reported to get better grades and perform better on standardised tests, leading to a lower dropout rate in grades eight through twelve. Furthermore, it has been postulated that high school sports can lead to higher levels of post-secondary education, especially for students with initially low test scores and low educational aspirations. Boys' participation in football or basketball, in particular, is associated with higher educational aspirations.

Finally, men who participated in high school sports are more productive workers and earn higher wages. According to the National Longitudinal Study of Youth, men at an average age of 32 who had played high school sports were paid wages 31% higher than those who did not.

All in all, sports can have a profound impact on a boy's physical, social, and academic development, as well as their future success in the workforce. Sport does help boys develop self-control, but only when other players and coaches model that emotional regulation is a strong part of the programme and where acting out is immediately and consistently disciplined. In some team sports, however, aggression is actually fostered, and therefore, emotional self-regulation is not emphasised as an important part of participating. Emotions such as sadness, grief and pain are often seen as unmanly and are not allowed to be expressed.

How does that look in action? As a teenager, one of my aims is for social acceptance. I want my peers to like me, really like me. So I'm good at a sport. This gives me a tribe; it gives me the opportunity to demonstrate that I'm good and deserving of their friendship and that, in exchange, I'm loyal to them. The price is that I have to undergo rituals and activities that involve harassment, abuse or humiliation as a way of being initiated. Once a member, my position is measured by my performance. If it drops, so does my popularity and status in the tribe. I could even get thrown out of the tribe, and therefore, I am open to coercive control.

As a man who is part of a team involved in sports, I may face various challenges. Suppose the team engages in destructive behaviours such as drug use and excessive drinking. In that case, it can be difficult to maintain my values and refrain from participating in those actions. Unfortunately, it is becoming increasingly common for males involved in sports at amateur and professional levels to face dangers and confrontations with authorities due to problems related to drugs, sexual behaviour, and gambling. These negative aspects are often a result of the intense focus on sports performance and status.

De Lench claims that men who played high school sports may be more productive, though the validity of this claim is uncertain. They likely receive higher pay, but it's worth considering whether this is due to their actual productivity or their perceived 'alpha' status by employers. Additionally, this phenomenon may be a result of nepotism and old-boy networks. These intriguing questions could be explored further, considering the potential influence of cognitive bias.

Patriarchal Families:

As a therapist, I often address the topic of family structure, which refers to how family relationships are organised. It involves understanding each family member's different roles and responsibilities and how they interact. In the case of heterosexual couples, the conventional model entails a primary partnership between the husband and wife, with children occupying a subordinate position in the family hierarchy. This model has been prevalent for centuries and passed down from generation to generation. However, as society evolves and progresses, we must question this model and its impact on family dynamics.

It's disheartening to realise that traditional patriarchal family models for heterosexual couples are still accepted as normal and appropriate in the twenty-first century. The model where the husband is seen as the head of the household continues to be considered by many in our community as normal. This traditional way of ordering the hierarchy within the family is based on false ideas about the capacities of men and women, which align with the seventeenth-century dualistic separation of the tasks of life into two distinct spheres. The man worked in the public sphere and didn't have the money to provide for the family. He was rational and, therefore, had the skills to determine how that money should be spent. The man, because he was seen as superior, also had the right to make all of the decisions about where the family would live and how they would live. The wife, who was seen as not naturally rational but emotionally driven, was biologically fitted for the domestic sphere, where she ran the home according to her husband's desires and raised the children. Women were treated as children rather than adults.

The failure to challenge this inherently unfair idea, that only one of the two adults in the marriage should be in charge, perpetuates both the subordination of women and gender stereotypes about how men and women should behave. It is at odds with the modern reality that women are legally and ethically considered to be autonomous and self-determining. It is at odds with the fact that most women continue to work and earn an income while married and raising their children, and it is at odds with the modern idea of a loving relationship between equals.

It takes very little imagination to see why this type of approach to marriage and family life would lead to conflict, resentment, stress and an unhealthy family environment. If children are raised to think that their talents and capacities are biologically determined, it undermines their belief in their right to choose how they want to live their lives. It also causes confusion when they become aware of the more egalitarian attitudes that now drive the expectations that others have of them. Another major problem with this sort of lopsided power distribution in the family is that it encourages dominance, with all of its negative potential for coercive control and domestic violence.

Marriage as a partnership requires cooperation and communication, with both partners sharing the decision-making and the tasks that lead to strong family bonds and a fulfilling family life. However, the traditional formulation of these partnerships is not only problematic for heterosexual couples. It excludes other, more diverse families and has been a major stumbling block in the path to acceptance of loving partnerships between non-heterosexual couples.

Patriarchy in Education: An Historical and Contemporary Lens

Throughout history, formal education has been used to maintain patriarchal structures and hierarchies. From the ancient world right through to the Enlightenment period in Europe, access to formal education was restricted to those who were part of particular groups. During much of European history, it was the priestly class that was educated, founded the universities, studied in them, and then disseminated that knowledge throughout the rest of society. Men from the ruling aristocratic families and rich merchants had access to literacy. However, the vast majority of men, and just about all women, were not universally literate, let alone educated.

One of the most important challenges that women identified as preventing them from being seen as equal was their lack of formal education. Women had little access, even when they belonged to the most wealthy and privileged sections of society. The prospect of educating women was seen as a subversive act that could destabilise men's entrenched power and status. Pioneering feminists identified this glaring inequity and took up the gauntlet to rectify it. Driven by the conviction that women possessed intellectual prowess equal to that of men, they waged a relentless campaign for equal educational prospects. Their advocacy bore fruit, culminating in women's expanded access to secondary and tertiary education and, eventually, in the mid-twentieth century, opening the doors to careers in traditionally male-dominated sectors like engineering and surgery. This constituted a watershed moment in the empowerment of women.

However, it's essential to recognise that the struggle for equitable education wasn't solely a women-centric endeavour. During the eighteenth and nineteenth centuries, the scope of formal education was the exclusive preserve of aristocratic and upper-class children, leaving working-class children of both sexes on the margins. As the Enlightenment progressed and ideas about equality and democracy were developed, education became an important feature of the new thinking about how societies should be governed. If all men were to be given the right to vote, they would need to be literate so that they could fully participate in the democratic process. It was the burgeoning movement for public education and universal literacy that finally democratised education, making it accessible to all strata of society.

While strides have been made, roadblocks continue to reduce the educational options of many men and women and their educational journeys are still hampered by inequality. The egalitarian project of the economic post-second-war period has been curtailed by the neoliberal approach to economics, and the resulting increase in inequity throughout the world has undermined educational opportunities for many in lower socio-economic demographics.

Based on empirical evidence, it remains unrealistic to presume that those with privilege and money will spontaneously upend their conventional roles and attitudes simply upon request. Moreover, it is unrealistic to expect men and women to sustain individual transformations within the architectures and institutions of a society that perpetuates the same hierarchical modalities.

For a transformative shift in social consciousness to occur, it is crucial for every social actor, particularly those wielding power, to converge on a unified objective. This mandates those at the apex of these power structures to willingly cede their entrenched privileges and engage collaboratively towards achieving common goals.

Within any hierarchical configuration, those who occupy dominant roles are likely to surrender their power only when perpetuating existing norms becomes unsustainable. Therefore, society at large must orchestrate this change, negating the need to rely solely on individuals' isolated initiatives. By fostering a collective commitment to change, we are better positioned to dismantle enduring hierarchies and realise an educational system that is genuinely equitable for all.

The Unseen Cost of Patriarchy: Educational Hierarchies and Their Impact on Boys and Secular Democracy

The fact is that the insidious reach of patriarchal systems extends beyond the suppression of women's opportunities; it also perpetuates harmful ideologies that have a detrimental impact on boys, moulding their emotional and intellectual development within narrowly defined limits.

The impact of patriarchal educational environments, particularly in private boys' schools, cannot be overlooked. These institutions are often characterised by rigid masculine norms that promote competitive aggression while scorning emotional vulnerability. The result is a culture that stifles emotional intelligence and promotes toxic masculinity, which perpetuates gender stereotypes and objectifies women. Unfortunately, this indoctrination can negatively affect the psychology of boys, leading to issues such as depression, anxiety, and poor self-esteem. Therefore, it is crucial to create educational environments that foster emotional intelligence and promote healthy masculinity to create a better future for everyone.

Beyond the immediate social and psychological impacts, these educational institutions also wield a broader, more systemic influence, particularly concerning the cultivation of democratic values in a secular society. Private boys' schools often reflect the social and political leanings of their patron communities, which can sometimes be traditionalist or even fundamentalist in nature. These schools become incubators for specific ideological perspectives, discouraging critical thinking and ideological diversity.

In a secular democracy, one of the critical educational goals is to develop citizens capable of critical thought, individuals who can participate in public discourse and decision-making in an informed, compassionate, and constructive manner. A patriarchal educational system—characterised by rigidity, hierarchy, and the suppression of dissenting voices—works antithetically to these democratic ideals. The result is a citizenry less equipped to engage in the pluralistic, multi-vocal discourse that is the hallmark of a healthy democracy.

Inculcating boys with the notion that their worth is tied to power, dominance, and emotional stoicism prepares them poorly for the responsibilities of civic life. It undermines the foundations of democratic equality by entrenching not only gender roles but divisive ideas about class and privilege, thus reinforcing power imbalances. Boys educated in such systems are less likely to question the status quo or challenge institutionalised inequalities, further perpetuating cycles of social and gender injustice.

To move towards a truly equitable and democratic society, we need to overhaul these patriarchal models that impede both male and female development. Our educational institutions must become arenas for empowerment, emotional growth, and critical inquiry, irrespective of gender. Only then can we cultivate a citizenry capable of sustaining a vibrant, inclusive, and secular democracy.

Patriarchy and the Neoliberal Economy

There is growing concern about the interconnectedness of politics, economic theory and commerce. These three areas of human activity have become a powerful and unwelcome trinity, each playing a crucial role in influencing the others. We have allowed ourselves to be convinced that these activities are more than tools that we, as a community, use to manage some aspects of our collective existence as a society. This triumvirate of power is totally focused on materialism and the constant exploitation of resources, both natural and human, and is, at its core, patriarchal. Neo-liberal economic theory, and let's remember it is a theory, the economy is not an entity or a god with a life of its own; it is a human construct, and it is aligned with all of the toxic values of patriarchy.

A journalist recently wrote an article about how mental health issues cost the economy billions of dollars. However, typical of how some in the media discuss important issues in today's world, his assertion lacked clarity and failed to consider causality. Factors such as economic insecurity, lack of job opportunities, and income inequality, along with the increasing divisions this causes in society, have contributed to the rise in anxiety, depression, and addiction (O'Donnell, 2018). When we look at the way in which the "economic imperative" has taken over in the last four decades and displaced what should be our primary focus as a community - our individual and collective well-being, it makes sense that there will be casualties.

Right now, as I write this, the Reserve Bank of Australia is trying to deal with inflation, and one of the problems preventing it from succeeding is that our unemployment rate is too low. Apparently, for the current economic theory to work, more people should be without an income. Let's be clear: that means no money for food and rent. You know, the basics. How can we, as a society, not see that this is a moral problem? Any economic theory that is predicated on the suffering of some of our neighbours is flawed.

The economic imperative refers to the idea that anything valuable is now solely defined in economic terms and references. Materialism has become the dominant measure of value. Money, property, possessions, and disposable income have become the top priorities in many people's minds, overshadowing other essential needs. However, research has shown that focusing on material possessions and monetary gain is linked to decreased well-being and increased mental health problems (Kasser, 2016).

Although it is essential to have a healthy and well-run economy, its role is to meet the needs of the whole community, and it should not be the sole measure of what we value. An equitable and morally just society prioritises the well-being of all its members because it recognises that all of us benefit when we do. Unfortunately, neo-liberal economic theory is predicated on the same four foundational values of patriarchy and just like patriarchy, it has had a profoundly negative impact on individuals and societies throughout the world.

One of the primary shared values in both these ideologies is the concept of exclusivity, which is territorial. In an unregulated free market, only those enterprises that can deliver power and wealth are valued, and only those who can carve out a space to garner that power and wealth are rewarded. This idea of exclusivity and the privilege it attracts marginalises everyone else. All those who are excluded from the spotlight are invisible and devalued.

This ties in with the second shared value of patriarchy, which is the hierarchy. Both patriarchy and neo-liberalism rely on hierarchical structures, with patriarchal systems positioning some men as superior, leading to their dominance in both public and private spheres. Neo-liberal ideologies create economic hierarchies, resulting in social stratification and systemic inequality. Women have historically been locked out of traditional social pathways to power and status, apart from being married into it, and they remain on the fringes. Those women who appear to have succeeded in those favoured enterprises that are viewed as economically important are few in number. They are also paid less, are more vulnerable to the brutal competitiveness of the market, and are required to be grateful for getting a seat at the table.

The values of territoriality and hierarchy are supported in action by the value of competitiveness and align with the value of acquisition. Both patriarchy and neo-liberalism are firmly nestled into the traditional masculine paradigm that promotes the relentless pursuit of power, wealth and status as a way of being accepted as a man. This competitive mindset views life as a zero-sum game which harms society, as it discourages cooperation, and instead fosters a culture of intense competition and division. In an environment where individuals are pitted against each other rather than working together towards common goals, it is impossible to form good quality supportive relationships. This, in turn, has a significant and negative impact on our personal identity, social interactions and ethical principles.

When it comes to individual identity, this intersection can be particularly challenging for men who feel pressured to conform to patriarchal ideals of masculinity, which are further complicated by neoliberalism's competitive ethos. This can lead to identity crises, mental health issues, and a sense of alienation from society.

In terms of social relations, the shared values of patriarchy and neo-liberalism shape social structures and influence the dynamics of social interactions. This can result in systemic injustices, prioritising materialism over altruism, and hinders cooperation due to competition. From a social perspective, this convergence can result in economic consequences such as income inequality, labour exploitation, and prioritising profit over the well-being of individuals and communities.

The intersection of these ideologies also calls into question the moral values of society. It encourages a pseudo-Darwinian struggle for survival and success, potentially eroding values such as empathy, compassion, and cooperation, which are fundamental to building a humane society. It is imperative to recognise and address the impact of these ideologies to create a more just and ethical society for all.

Over time, our expectations of politicians have become more narrow, solely focused on their ability to manage the economy. With the economy becoming the centrepiece of our society, politicians have adapted their roles to fit into this structure. It is crucial that we as a community reimagine our priorities so that the economy is only one of the important issues that our representatives attend to. Social justice, environmental stewardship, and safeguarding human rights are equally significant. By raising our expectations of our leaders and making them accountable to a more comprehensive set of values and principles, we can establish a fairer and more sustainable society for everyone.

One of the more significant consequences of the way our moral values have been highjacked by neo-liberal economics is that the idea of political service to the community has been lost. What was once a role taken on by those who wanted to serve the community for a period of time has instead become a profession. The rise of professional politicians, still mostly men, has led to a self-serving class of individuals. Their education and occupational history are just training grounds for their political careers, which means they have little, if any, understanding of other sections of society. They work within an adversarial and competitive environment from the time they join one of the political parties, usually at university. Politics is fundamentally hierarchical, and its core aim is to grasp and maintain power, both as individuals and, for the majority of politicians, for their party.

The major political parties have become unstable due to their focus being on the short period in which they are in power. All of their interests are concentrated on maintaining that power, and along with the now professionalised member of parliament, these parties are no longer anchored to their traditional social values or bases. In Tony Benn's words, they have become the weathercocks. Weathercocks will spin in whatever direction the wind of public opinion may blow them, no matter what principal they may have to compromise.

When leaders lack values and a sustainable vision for society, they can create a society focused solely on economic growth and commerce. This can result in a society where individuals constantly struggle to make ends meet as they navigate an ever-changing occupational landscape driven by one institution: business and its financial interests. In such a society, people often feel alienated and disconnected and divided from each other, as their survival becomes their priority. This financial impoverishment inevitably undermines people's capacity to pursue personal goals and achieve true agency in their lives.

If we step back from the microcosm of our own society and look at this from a planetary perspective, we can see that the patriarchal values that drive our current economic system has far-reaching and seriously dangerous consequences. In many developing countries, leaders with a narrow focus on economic growth have pursued policies that prioritise the interests of multinational corporations over the needs of their own citizens. This has resulted in the exploitation of natural resources, environmental degradation, and the displacement of local communities. In these situations, individuals are often left with no choice but to work in low-paying jobs with little job security or benefits, as their governments prioritise the interests of foreign investors over their own people.

In more developed countries, similar trends emerge as leaders prioritise short-term economic growth over long-term sustainability. This can lead to the erosion of social safety nets, rising income inequality, and a lack of investment in education and healthcare. As a result, individuals are left to fend for themselves in an increasingly competitive and unforgiving economic environment, where the only priority is profit.

Overall, it is clear that leaders who are captive to patriarchal values and who have no sustainable vision for the well-being of all the members of their society can, and do, profoundly impact the lives of individuals and the health of our social and environmental ecology. It is up to all of us to demand more from our leaders and hold them accountable for their choices. We must prioritise the well-being of our communities and the health of our planet rather than the interests of a select few.

Many people have lost faith in the political system, which seems only to benefit those in power or with economic advantages. In the US and most other nations where voting is optional, this has resulted in declining voter turnout as people feel their votes won't make a difference. This reinforces existing social hierarchies based on wealth and power in Western democracies.

In the context of the topic of masculinity, these social factors are a vital part of the picture as they contribute to the feelings of disenfranchisement, irrelevance, and disillusionment that many men experience. These emotions can stem from various sources, such as economic instability, changes in traditional gender roles, and a sense of powerlessness in one's personal and professional life. For instance, some studies have shown that men who have been laid off or are struggling to find work may feel a sense of emasculation and loss of identity. This may be compounded by the fact that traditional male-dominated industries, such as manufacturing and mining, are declining in many parts of the world.

Additionally, changes in gender roles and expectations can leave many men uncertain about their place in society. For example, men who were raised to believe their role was to be the primary breadwinner for their family may feel lost and adrift when that expectation is no longer feasible or desirable. It's important to note that these feelings of frustration and helplessness are not unique to men. However, some men may be more likely to channel their anger and resentment towards groups they perceive as having taken their rightful place or opportunities from them. This can lead to harmful behaviours such as misogyny, racism, and xenophobia.

As a society, it's important that we acknowledge and address these underlying issues to create a more equitable and inclusive world. This can involve supporting policies that promote economic theories that enable equity and stability, educating ourselves about the social construction of traditional gender roles and expectations, and combating discrimination and prejudice in all its forms. By doing so, we can create a world where all individuals, regardless of gender, race, or other factors, can thrive and reach their full potential.

Status Anxiety: Why Social Issues Become Psychological 'Disorders.'

Observing a group of boys, particularly those in adolescence, demonstrates some common patterns of behaviour. These boys establish a designated area, often referred to as their turf, and subsequently establish a hierarchy amongst themselves. This hierarchy is often based on physical attributes, with the most developed individuals typically rising to the top. In gang scenarios, this often involves the boys who can instil the greatest sense of fear through physical strength or who can manipulate the group's perception of other members. The desire for inclusion and acceptance creates a fear of rejection that all members experience.

This is because we are inculcated from very early in our lives to want to be part of the group and because of the entrenched patriarchy within our societies, we always assume that any group must have a leader. The followers are also usually ordered into some sort of hierarchy. Irrespective of where they are in that group, most of the members will desire to improve their status. At the same time they don't want to lose what status they already have. This is an example of what Alain de Botton talks about as Status Anxiety.

De Botton is a philosopher who recognised that this particular type of anxiety stems from our being overly preoccupied with how others perceive our success within the narrow context of what is considered socially valuable in modern affluent societies. He noted that the desire of many people to climb the social ladder and to be seen as successful made them vulnerable to anxiety and other forms of emotional distress when they feel that they have failed.

In a society that follows a patriarchal system, people who do not conform to the established hierarchy are often considered insignificant. The expectation to evaluate one's self-worth based on one's rank in the social ladder can cause anxiety and depression, especially for those who think they have a chance of being at the top but don't make it. When the only way to achieve status is through the accumulation of territory, wealth and power there are only a few who can actually achieve this status. When there are no alternative ways to be valued, those who do not have access to the resources or whose talents and skills are not valued can become disappointed, and this can lead to depression and self-destructive behaviours like addictions.

So, what do men do to cope with this? We become acquisitional. In the modern world of unregulated capitalism, there is a myth that there are unlimited resources out there. All it takes for the individual to get their share, or actually far more than their share, is that they make the right choices about their education and occupation and work hard. In this fairytale, the accumulation of wealth and possessions will make you happy and give you social status.

The notion that material possessions can bring us happiness is not a novel concept. In fact, the Roman statesman and philosopher Seneca questioned this idea more than two thousand years ago. It is a curious coincidence that this observation came from a Roman, a member of a society characterised by wealth and power. Rome was a patriarchal society that emphasised the acquisition of territory, wealth, and influence. The idea of pursuing these goals was deeply ingrained in the fabric of Roman society.

Seneca says, "For many men, the acquisition of wealth does not end their troubles; it only changes them." Acquiring something can refer to obtaining, gaining, procuring, or earning it, but being acquisitive can also imply a sense of avarice. The way in which something is acquired is related to its value, our emotional attachment to it, and how it is received. It's important to note that the term "acquire" is not used when referring to people. For example, you would not acquire a spouse unless you live in a society where it is possible to purchase one. While you might not use the term "acquire" when obtaining a degree or a friend, it may be used when obtaining an object such as a car, house, or other material possessions. This concept of acquisition and its relationship to emotional attachment and value is explored in various fields, including psychology and economics. For example, studies have shown that individuals who place high value on material possessions are more likely to experience negative emotions and have lower levels of well-being (Belk, 1985; Kasser, 2002).

Additionally, research has found that the way in which people acquire wealth can impact their psychological well-being, with those who inherit wealth experiencing higher levels of anxiety and depression compared to those who earn their wealth (Griffin & Hesketh, 2004). These findings support the long held understanding of many people that pursuing material possessions and wealth may not necessarily lead to greater happiness or fulfilment. The old adage that 'you can't take it with you' is a common sense expression that possessions do not lead to happiness.

Since the Agricultural Revolution, property ownership has served two main purposes. First, it allowed some individuals or families to increase their assets and social status by showcasing their wealth. Second, it provides a means to control resources and further advance that individual's or family's position in the social hierarchy, leading to more opportunities for acquisition. As a result, those in lower social positions have learnt that to elevate their social standing, they need to strive to acquire more assets.

Our culture and traditions have been shaped by ideas passed down through history. We have inherited the Roman tradition that was established to build an empire. These ideas have evolved over time and contributed to the world's current geopolitical and economic state. Such beliefs are not unique to the Romans and can be found in all human societies. The belief that financial and social success leads to happiness is a strong conviction.

Over the centuries, Capitalism and Consumerism have evolved alongside the quest for individual freedom and equality, which has disrupted traditional social hierarchies. As a result, individuals who were once excluded by their class or family background can now pursue social mobility through wealth. However, this has also led to people struggling to maintain their identity amidst changing family structures and endless consumer choices. It appears that the more possessions we accumulate, the more we crave.

When we place excessive value on material possessions and prioritise the acquisition of wealth and its trappings, it creates a distorted perception of the importance of things. Our culture has become fixated on accumulating material goods and the status they represent to the owner. As a result, many individuals experience feelings of disconnection and isolation as they prioritise financial gain and prestige over nurturing strong social bonds. This has led to a widespread issue of loneliness among many people. There is a lot of evidence that the ongoing increase in mental health problems amongst the most affluent societies is a result of this over-valuing of the material facets of our lives and the devaluing of the non-material. The economic imperative, with its hierarchical and status-based evaluations, is socially divisive, and studies have shown a correlation between income inequality and poor mental health outcomes [Wilkinson & Pickett, 2010].

In addition, affluence itself may be responsible for the deterioration of our physical health. The constant pursuit of wealth and material possessions can lead to unhealthy lifestyles, such as overconsumption of unhealthy foods and lack of exercise (Wilkinson & Pickett, 2010). Recognising that a physically and mentally healthy society requires more than just access to healthcare is crucial. Addressing systemic economic and social inequalities is also essential for promoting overall well-being (Marmot, 2005).

This can all sound somewhat counterintuitive. How could increased affluence be such a problem? The overall level of prosperity in our society, as well as in other Western societies, has surpassed any historical precedent. While certain groups within our communities still continue to be marginalised and disconnected from the significant advancements in living standards made over the last century, most Western countries have established a governmental welfare system or a "safety net" to aid the most financially disadvantaged. However, what we are seeing socially and psychologically, in our mental health statistics and in our lived experience, is the loss of the importance of all the other aspects of our lives as humans. It's not affluence that is bad for us; it is the way we have created it and the way we have distributed it amongst ourselves.

The desire for material possessions is not new; there were always people prepared to sacrifice anything and everything to acquire them. What is new is the linking of the status gained from accumulating wealth with the idolisation of the individual. The particular characterisation of the individual that we have seen emerge over the last few decades is the one that has become disconnected from the community and the obligations of society. This idea that we are atomised, abstract and alone was very much the type of person Ayn Rand promoted in her 'Objectivism' philosophy. Her thinking was a very important influence on those who not only developed neo-liberal economics but those who promoted it during the 1980s. Ayn Rand believed that the only moral objective the individual should have is to pursue their own happiness through rational self-interest. She argued that laissez-faire capitalism, which we now call the free market economy, is the only social system that enables individuals to achieve this objective.

However, while capitalism may promote individual freedom and autonomy, we now have proof that unregulated capitalism leads to increased inequality, the erosion of the middle class and social unrest, and not just in developing nations or nations with underdeveloped democracies. In fact, since the political system of democracy is underpinned by a robust and sizeable middle class, the fact that it is shrinking in many Western nations is a significantly damaging consequence of this type of radical individualistic approach to life.

To address these concerns, some propose alternative economic models, such as socialism or democratic socialism, prioritising social welfare and income equality. These models emphasise the need for collective action and redistribution of resources to ensure that everyone has access to basic needs and opportunities for upward mobility. The discussion about various economic models reflects deeper philosophical inquiries about the government's role, human motivation, and happiness. Finding a definitive answer is challenging, but weighing the ethical consequences of our economic decisions and working towards a society that values individual freedom and fairness is crucial.

Hang on a minute, you might say; rational selfishness can work. Hmm, really?

Renowned author Gore Vidal once criticised Ayn Rand's "philosophy" as deeply immoral. Rand's belief that "The first right on earth is the right of the ego. Man's first duty is to himself" highlights her lack of concern for the interconnectedness of human beings in society. Rand's philosophy is based on the concept of the independent individual who inherently possesses "rights." However, in reality, our "rights" are granted to us by each other in the context of our relationships and our position as members of society.

Vidal's criticism of Rand's philosophy is based on the moral impoverishment of her ideas and the realities of human life. Her belief that individuals should prioritise their own self-interest above all else ignores the fact that we live in a society where our actions impact others. She completely failed to acknowledge or recognise that humans are a 'connected species'[Williams, 2023], and that we need each other to live emotionally and psychologically healthy lives. Her version of self-interest is predicated on the instrumental use of others for your own advantage.

Our individual rights are an essential component of a functioning society. However, these rights are not absolute and must be balanced with the needs and rights of others. Rand's philosophy fails to recognise the importance of social responsibility. In society, it is our duty to contribute to the betterment of our community and help those who are less fortunate. Rand's philosophy promotes a selfish individualism that ignores the needs of others, which ultimately contributes to social inequality.

The devaluation of non-economic aspects of life, such as the Arts, Humanities, and other intangible values, has hurt the global economic landscape. This trend has led to anti-intellectualism, prioritising vocational education and the mercantile world. Moral concerns such as fair wages, parental leave, and helping the less fortunate who continue to struggle even in societies with abundant resources, have been sidelined by the economic imperative. This acquisitive, materialistic drive is unsustainable, not only from a social perspective but also from a resources and existential perspective. It is a quintessential reflection of the entrenched patriarchal ideology that dominates every aspect of our lives.

Despite these challenges, there are signs of hope and progress. A growing number of individuals and organisations are advocating for a more balanced and holistic approach to economic and social development, one that takes into account the needs and aspirations of all members of society, as well as the health of our planet. However, in order to do this successfully we need to recognise that we cannot thrive if we don't do our best to ensure that all of us have a chance to meet our essential needs for survival.

In 1943, Abraham Maslow, a psychologist, reaffirmed the common sense understanding that humans have essential needs that must be met for optimal functioning. Using his expertise and research, he categorised these requirements into a pyramid hierarchy. The foundation of this pyramid comprises our physical necessities, including food, water, clothing, and shelter, which are crucial for our survival. These are our most critical and vital needs, along with a sense of safety. These needs are met initially within our families with the support of the community in which we live. Maslow's hierarchy of needs emphasises the importance of personal safety against harm, accidents, and illness as a fundamental requirement. At the heart of this hierarchy of human needs is the need for social connections and a sense of belonging. This need is fulfilled by establishing close relationships with family, friends and romantic partners. Studies in psychology and sociology have shown that humans possess an inherent desire to be loved and to feel connected to others. This need for emotional connection is critical to overall happiness and well-being. When this need is not met, individuals may experience negative emotions such as loneliness, anxiety, and depression. Indeed, research has suggested that social isolation and loneliness can have significant negative effects on both physical and mental health. For example, people who lack social connections are at a greater risk of developing heart disease, high blood pressure, and other ailments. Additionally, loneliness has been linked to an increased risk of depression, anxiety, and other mental health disorders.

This sense of safety also extends to our financial security as we need to adequately provide for ourselves and our loved ones. It's crucial to recognise that these are necessities and not mere desires. Unfortunately, in today's society, financial security is often equated with more than what is genuinely necessary for an individual or a family. This often leads both men and women to prioritise their paid work over the other areas of their lives. There are many people in our community who appear to have met all of the status goals required by the four values of patriarchy but are desperately lonely and unhappy, as they have no time left for anything else. The increase in mental health problems in our community is a consequence of this lack of balance.

Given the importance of social connections to overall well-being, it is important for individuals to actively seek out and nurture personal and social relationships. This can involve joining social groups or clubs, reaching out to friends and family members regularly, and making an effort to meet new people and form new connections. By prioritising social connections and investing time and energy into building and maintaining relationships, individuals can improve their overall quality of life and achieve greater happiness and fulfilment.

Maslow's hierarchy of needs highlights the second level as the desire for esteem, which encompasses feeling respected and valued by oneself and others. However, it's essential to acknowledge that seeking validation solely from others can sometimes negatively impact one's overall well-being. Maslow emphasises that self-respect, rooted in personal satisfaction and inner competence, is a higher need and more significant for individuals.

At the top of the pyramid of needs is the need to achieve self-actualisation. Self-actualisation is a complex and multifaceted concept that has been the subject of much discussion and debate in psychology. At its core, self-actualisation involves reaching one's full potential and living a fulfilling and meaningful life. This involves a deep understanding of oneself and one's unique talents, interests, and capacities. One of the key components of self-actualisation is self-discovery. This involves exploring one's innermost thoughts, feelings, and desires, as well as one's strengths and weaknesses. Through this process, individuals can gain greater self-awareness and a deeper understanding of what they truly want out of life.

Self-reflection is also an important aspect of self-actualisation. This involves taking the time to reflect on one's experiences and learn from them. By reflecting on past successes and failures, individuals can gain valuable insights into their own strengths and weaknesses and use this knowledge to make better decisions in the future.

Finally, self-realisation is a key component of self-actualisation. This involves putting one's unique talents and abilities to work in pursuit of one's goals and aspirations. By tapping into one's creativity, spirituality, and intellectual capacities, individuals can achieve a sense of purpose and fulfilment that is unmatched by any other pursuit.

Striving to achieve our personal best requires fulfilling our basic needs first. It's not a matter of achieving perfection but broadening our awareness and figuring out how we define our potential at the highest level of the pyramid. Men commonly assess their value based on their occupation, social status or financial situation, often influenced by patriarchal norms. Nevertheless, it is crucial to acknowledge that self-fulfilment as an individual encompasses various other aspects, such as self-awareness, emotional intelligence, positive relationships, and overall well-being.

However, there is a caveat. If you don't have the first level of the pyramid covered, you have no chance at self-actualisation. The values of patriarchy remain entrenched in our societies. Although there was a brief period post the Second World War when the old class divisions were challenged, and a more egalitarian ideal was promoted in Western Democracies, it didn't last. Patriarchy fought back.

The impact of the social and economic changes that have taken place over the last few decades has been devastating for middle-class individuals, both men and women alike. While working longer hours, they have less job security than ever. The result is a growing sense of anxiety and uncertainty about the future. The elite political class often promotes and justifies greed and avarice, which is prevalent in the halls of power. Superpowers' military-industrial complexes have transformed wars into business opportunities, while organised crime flourishes within legitimate spheres of influence and the mainstream economy. These illicit operations have expanded their influence across continents and societies, dividing the world to maximise profits from unlawful activities.

To make matters worse, our personal liberties are still being curtailed by a select group of politicians and businesspeople who use tax loopholes to enrich themselves at our expense. This leaves many feeling powerless and disenfranchised, unable to make meaningful changes to their own lives. Meanwhile, environmental degradation continues to be a pressing concern. Despite growing awareness of the need for sustainable practices and conservation efforts, the insatiable greed of the wealthy few persists, leading to continued environmental exploitation and destruction.

I believe that the evidence is overwhelmingly strong that patriarchy is no longer only exploiting women, children and the disadvantaged but is now exploiting most men. We have 'drunk the Kool-Aid.' For those of you unfamiliar with this phase, it refers to a person or group holding an unquestioned belief, argument, or philosophy without critical examination. It originated after an event in November 1978 in a place called Jonestown where over 900 members of the Peoples Temple, who were followers of Jim Jones, committed suicide by drinking a mixture of a powdered soft drink flavouring agent laced with cyanide.

We have drunk the Kool-Aid. Unlike Maslow's hierarchy, the Patriarchal hierarchy, along with territorial and acquisitional attitudes, behaviours and values, has influenced our culture so deeply that it has had major negative consequences for individuals, both male and female, and the communities we live in. There has been, at least since the agricultural revolution, an attitude of forever growing and expanding, a sort of human big bang that has rapidly spread across the planet. Unfortunately, there is no unlimited expansion of any kind. Even the universe, at some point, will reverse its expansion and begin to collapse into itself.

It's common for men to feel overwhelmed and powerless when it comes to addressing important issues. But we can all make a difference, starting with ourselves and our relationships and eventually impacting the world as a whole. Throughout history, we have seen that one individual can significantly impact the world, either for better or worse. 'Making Good Men Great' is based on the idea that we can revolutionise the way we think about ourselves, gender dynamics, and society by starting locally and expanding globally.

As Nelson Mandela once said, things may seem impossible until achieved. This situation is no exception. The choice is yours. Even if you only change yourself, you can make a difference. However, before we dive into what it means to be exceptional, there's one more issue to address: the problematic aspects of patriarchy and conventional masculinity in our personal and social lives.

At a granular level, patriarchal constructs insidiously infiltrate the individual's psyche. In our quest to navigate social norms, we often find ourselves trapped within the narrow constraints of prescribed gender roles, stunting our emotional growth and authenticity. This issue of gender has become confusing and worrying to many people who do not understand the way the concept is being used in today's world. It is important to remember that "GENDER IS A SOCIAL CONSTRUCT". It ignores the actual talents, preferences and interests of the human being and dictates their way of being in the world according to their genitalia. This affects all of us [Ford, C, 2018, p17].

Men, in particular, face the burden of embodying "masculine" traits. These normative expectations, which equate masculinity with emotional stoicism, physical strength, and aggressive competition, effectively shrink the allowable emotional spectrum for men. As documented in "Conformity to Masculine Norms and Psychological Distress" (Wong, Ho, Wang & Miller, 2017), adherence to these rigid gender norms has been strongly linked with psychological distress. This suppressed emotional range manifests in many mental health challenges, including depression and anxiety.

Similarly, research such as the work of Seidler et al., 2016, highlights the association between adherence to traditional masculine norms and poorer mental health, including a higher likelihood of depressive symptoms. It further points out that men who endorse these norms are less likely to seek help, which can lead to dire consequences in the context of mental health. Indeed, one of the most tragic ramifications of these constraints is the high rate of suicide among men.

The social expectation for men to "bear their burdens silently" often discourages them from seeking help when grappling with psychological distress. This grim reality is reflected in data from the American Foundation for Suicide Prevention, which indicates that men died by suicide 3.63 times more often than women in 2019. Similarly, the World Health Organisation corroborates this, finding notably higher suicide rates among men in high-income countries.

Hyper-masculinity is an exaggerated form of masculinity associated with aggression, dominance, and a disregard for emotions and vulnerability. This concept has been studied extensively in various fields, including psychology, sociology, and gender studies. Some examples of hyper-masculine behaviour include excessive competitiveness, sexual objectification of women, and a tendency to use violence to solve problems.

Research has shown that hyper-masculinity can have negative consequences for both men and women. Men who adhere to hyper-masculine norms may experience high stress and anxiety levels as they constantly feel pressure to prove their masculinity. On the other hand, women may be objectified and marginalised by hyper-masculine men, leading to feelings of powerlessness and insecurity.

The impact of hyper-masculinity on young men and the community at large can be quite devastating. It is important to question whether or not individuals identify with the aggressor and whether they model themselves on men who represent power, aggression, and dominance as a 'god-given' right. This can be particularly tempting for those who feel disempowered, disenfranchised, and ambitious. However, without proper guidance, this kind of mindset can perpetuate the very problems we are currently facing.

To combat hyper-masculinity, promoting a more inclusive and positive understanding of masculinity is important. This can be done by emphasising empathy, emotional intelligence, and cooperation and discouraging harmful behaviours such as aggression and sexual harassment. By taking a 'Big History of Men' approach, we can recognise the diversity of masculinities throughout history and cultures and work towards creating a more equitable and respectful society for everyone. Men are born into, and live in families. The characterisation of men as separate and abstracted from their connections to others is a result of patriarchy's vice-grip upon family dynamics, which cannot be overstated. Rooted in antiquated power imbalances, it disturbs the equilibrium within households and fosters an environment rife with inequality and resentment. Such dynamics are not merely abstract concepts but tangible realities documented extensively in socio-cultural research and reports. The consequences are felt by many people who live unhappy lives, unable to sustain intimate and supportive relationships, because their expectations of themselves and their partners are unrealistic and unfair.

This often leads to men's alienation within the familial structure. Often conditioned to be the provider rather than a nurturer, men may find themselves emotionally disconnected from their families, becoming "absent" fathers or partners. This emotional distancing can lead to feelings of loneliness and abandonment for their children, as noted by Nielsen in "Father-Daughter Relationships: Contemporary Research and Issues" (2012).

Moreover, patriarchal values also give rise to more sinister forms of control within family settings: intimate partner violence and coercive control. Such violence isn't limited to physical assault but can encompass emotional abuse, sexual coercion, economic manipulation, and psychological domination, as illustrated by Stark in "Coercive Control" (2007). This omnipresent dread, caused by controlling behaviours, inflicts profound emotional and psychological damage on victims, with devastating effects on familial harmony and individual mental health.

Children, the often silent witnesses to such power dynamics, bear the psychological brunt. Exposure to violence and controlling behaviours can lead to an array of long-term effects, including anxiety, depression, and post-traumatic stress disorder (PTSD), as noted in the seminal study "The Impact of Exposure to Domestic Violence on Children and Young People: A Review of the Literature" (Holt, Buckley, & Whelan, 2008).

According to the Australian Bureau of Statistics, in 2019, the suicide rate for men was three times higher than that of women. In the UK, the rate of suicide among men is also significantly higher than that of women, with men accounting for three-quarters of all suicides. These statistics highlight the urgent need for society to address toxic masculine norms and promote help-seeking behaviour and emotional vulnerability among men. Creating a safe and supportive environment for men to seek help and support when needed, without fear of judgment or stigma.

Society as a whole bears the scars of patriarchal systems. Economic, educational, and legal structures have been moulded to reflect these values. The workplace and the world of business have been prioritised and have been consistently designed to deny the value of family and individual well-being. Women remain underrepresented in positions of power and authority and are expected to carry the burden of all of the tasks of life that patriarchy fails to value. The very fact that those domestic and caring tasks are vitally necessary and have been calculated to be worth hundreds of billions of dollars of the world's GDP is completely ignored.

On the political front, patriarchal norms have long shaped the corridors of power, sidelining men who do not adhere to patriarchal norms as well as women, thus subverting democratic principles. Despite some progress, women are woefully underrepresented in political offices worldwide, with data from the Inter-Parliamentary Union revealing a mere 25.5% of all national parliamentarians being women as of 2021. Furthermore, patriarchal influences colour policy decisions, often marginalising issues disproportionately affecting women, such as reproductive rights and gender-based violence.

In short, the deeply rooted ideology of patriarchy not only propagates many injustices but also exacts a staggering toll on mental health. It is incumbent upon society to challenge these outdated norms, fostering an environment that supports all individuals' holistic well-being and equality. In the opening section of this book, I painted a picture of how patriarchy has negatively impacted men's well-being across all aspects of life. I also made the case that expecting men to change is futile without addressing the social systems surrounding them. That our efforts must go beyond individual change and encompass systemic political, social, and cultural changes.

It's imperative that we acknowledge the detrimental effects of being territorial, hierarchical, acquisition-driven and competitive in our society. If we continue to operate in this manner, we cannot expect to succeed meaningfully. Patriarchy is a pervasive issue that needs to be addressed from within the male community. It's time to move beyond the confines of one discipline like psychology, sociology, or history and approach the problem from a multidisciplinary platform.

To truly understand men's physical, psychological, social, and spiritual challenges, we must listen to their experiences and address the issues at the root of the problem. Our statistics in all these areas indicate a crisis, and it's time we address this call to action. There is a complex relationship between individuals and their environment, and yes, despite calls for individual men to take responsibility for their actions, our institutions continue to operate as they always have. However, we are not powerless. We can start by being the best person we can be. By rejecting the binary mentality of gender stereotypes and reshaping our understanding of our own masculinity, we can enhance our own well-being. As more of us take control of the dialogue and demonstrate the benefits of changing from good to great, others will recognise that they, too, can find a better way of being a man in today's world.

A New Masculinity
   Let's Reimagine Masculinity

Overview

In this section of the book, I would like to discuss how we can progress. While it is true that most men are good people who do not exhibit violent behaviour towards women and children or anyone else, there is still a significant number of men who intimidate, threaten, and act aggressively towards others. Other men, women and children are the victims of these men, and they can be found in all professions, occupations and levels of society, including in positions of political and institutional power. Furthermore, some men who lack influence or power and seek ways to better their situation are vulnerable to these men's influence. As I launched Making Good Men Great, my project and movement had three primary objectives. Firstly, to reimagine the concept of masculinity. Second, to develop a comprehensive curriculum that facilitates change in men; and third, to assist men in building supportive networks that aid them in their journey. To enhance our lives as individuals, we must recognise the tasks ahead of us on the road to self-discovery. This includes considering our beliefs and behaviours towards our family, friends, work colleagues, and acquaintances. We need to examine how we interact with all facets of our lives and our community, and just like with any other journey, we need to have an idea of where we are heading. We need to ask ourselves what legacy we will leave behind. How will we be remembered by those who knew us and those we love? Will I be remembered as a good or great person, and by what measure?

In the first section of this book, we identified the core issue that causes harm to both women and men in human societies. Patriarchy is so entrenched in our thinking and our social institutions that we often don't recognise its dangerous influence. We express ourselves in ways that normalise the negative, divisive and harmful ideas of territoriality, hierarchy, acquisition and competitiveness without consciously realising it. But our children are listening, and they hear and internalise these ideas.

It is important to reiterate the words of Edmund Burke, who stated that "the only thing necessary for the triumph of evil is for good men to do nothing." However, simply being a good person may not be enough. Should we strive for greatness, and if so, can we achieve it alone, or should we unite with women who have long been at the forefront of the fight against patriarchy?

Moreover, we must challenge the conventional definition of greatness, which is often tied to traditional masculine ideals and hyper-masculinity. To do this, we need a clear framework that allows men to engage in personal and social evolution that fosters convergence with women and those who do not fit the stereotypical mould—a framework that acknowledges that human persons are not, and should not be, defined and restrained by narrow stereotypes.

Psychologically speaking, our development has been stunted in adolescence, hindering us from reaching emotional maturity as adults. We are trapped in a perpetual state of adolescence, which is meant to be a temporary transition to adulthood, not a permanent lifestyle. This confinement makes males reactive, defensive, and inflexible instead of being responsive, open, and capable of gracefully managing life's stresses. In engineering terms, this means that we are prone to breaking when stress levels reach a critical point. To redefine masculinity, we must reimagine ourselves as mature and responsible human beings rather than being trapped in the patriarchal mindset that keeps us stuck in adolescence. Patriarchy has caused harm, and we must work towards a new way of being that is inclusive and progressive.

A Masculinity for a New Future

These are the values I want to propose to form the basis of a New Masculinity that we can incorporate into our daily lives. These values shape our expectations, relationships, and perspective towards the world and those around us. The New Masculinity emphasises -

inclusivity over territoriality,
    democracy over hierarchy,
    distribution over acquisition, and

cooperation over competition. Let me further explain these principles.

These are the values that enabled us as a species to survive and thrive in the first place. Without our ability to cooperate with each other in an inclusive, egalitarian and fair manner, we would never have made it out of the African savanna. We evolved to be this way, and so it is no surprise that abandoning these characteristics of ourselves has caused us significant harm [Williams, M. *The Connected Species*, 2023].

Being Inclusive:

Incorporating inclusivity into our daily lives is a valuable framework that encourages us to rethink our automatic reactions and respond thoughtfully in the way we manage our lives. By adopting an "and/also" perspective instead of a divisive "either/or" approach, we can avoid being swayed by arbitrary dichotomies or polarities like "us vs them" or "I" vs "the other." This change in mindset is crucial in combating issues such as discrimination, racism, sexism, and class divisions that can arise in groups, communities, and societies. Inclusivity also encourages us to consider ideas and issues from a broader perspective, laying the foundation for equality and respect.

Inclusivity is also important in forming good quality, supportive, and loving relationships. It is the foundation for human intimacy and is, therefore, crucial to our wellbeing and happiness. This change in perspective has enormous benefits for us as individuals. For example, recently, I had the opportunity to work with a couple who I will call John and Jenny. They felt that their relationship had become stagnant and lacked shared interests despite their love for each other.

Their financial stability allowed Jenny to choose to focus on maintaining their home while John pursued a demanding corporate career. They maintained traditional stereotypical gender roles, and John often spent his free time with his male friends, while Jenny had close relationships with her female friends. Even their vacations were divided into 'his' and 'hers'. They seldom shared their personal lives with each other, assuming that the other party would not be interested.

It may be apparent to some of you what the problem is here, but John and Jenny were unable to see it. They had a tendency to act independently of each other, which is a common trait in the couples I work with. To them, it was just how things were. However, this resulted in the relationship becoming less emotional and increasingly pragmatic, and it was beginning to stall. If we look at what was happening in their lives from a patriarchal perspective, they both had very strictly defined territories of operation. They not only divided up the tasks of life into two separate spheres of operation, but they erected strong boundaries around those spheres and excluded each other. They basically lived separate lives.

Once they realised that to strengthen their relationship, they would need to be more interdependent and inclusive, they decided to make some simple and practical changes in the way they interacted with each other. The focus of these changes was to help them appreciate the significance of including each other in their lives.

Despite not always seeing eye-to-eye or agreeing on everything, John and Jenny respected each other enough and valued their relationship enough to work together. By including each other in their plans and activities and sharing experiences, they were able to rediscover their feelings for one another. This sharing of their daily lives allowed them to come closer and strengthen their bond.

Being Democratic:

Many people frequently inquire about my rationale for incorporating the concept of democracy as one of the core values for 'Making Good Men Great'. However, once we reflect on the philosophical ideas behind democracy, it makes sense to embrace this way of thinking on both a personal and social level. After all, democracy is based on the belief that every human being is of equal worth, regardless of race, ethnicity, religion or any other ideology they might identify with. One of the defining characteristics of democracy is its emphasis on valuing differences. It demands that we acknowledge and tolerate the diversity that exists among individuals as a way of demonstrating respect towards them. By treating others respectfully, we create an environment where we can expect to be treated likewise. This fundamental concept has had far-reaching effects on our society, influencing every facet of our personal, organisational, and political lives.

If we reflect on how being democratic in the way in which we relate to others looks in reality, we can easily see how different it is to patriarchy, which is exclusive and divisive and underpins other prevalent political ideologies such as Marxism, Communism, dictatorships and hereditary monarchies. As we have seen in the discussion in Section One, patriarchy is centred around the belief that some men are superior and should have power over everyone else. Remember, the patriarch is the father figure in charge, and this is the basis of autocracy and is underpinned by the belief that 'might gives me the right'.

Despite our having embraced democratic thinking over the last few hundred years, the power of patriarchy remains deeply ingrained and is not limited to conscious beliefs. Although most men may not necessarily subscribe to patriarchal beliefs on a conscious level, our socialisation has left us susceptible to a subconscious influence on our thoughts, feelings, and actions. This leaves us essentially unaware of our patriarchal tendencies, thus highlighting the significance of acknowledging and addressing such tendencies.

An example of how we can use democratic ideals in our everyday lives is how teenagers can use democratic principles as they develop their individuality without losing connection with their peer group. My primary focus in my work with teens is to assist them in making ethical decisions independently, without giving in to the pressures of their peers. This concept in adults translates to showing tolerance towards an individual's unique perspective, fostering constructive conversations and dialogues. Stereotypical judgments are avoided, and people are viewed objectively, which can help eliminate gender and race biases and power dynamics often referred to as hegemonic.

Being Distributive

Being distributive is the opposite of being aquisitional. When we are acquisition, we are looking to gather resources, material goods, or even people for ourselves for our own exclusive use. We are driven to own rather than share. This desire not to share doesn't only apply to material goods; it applies to sharing our space, sharing of ourselves, our knowledge and skills, our time and our emotions.

The concept of distribution plays a vital role in the idea of sharing what we have with others. It is an essential component of generosity, and it allows us to appreciate our good fortune and develop a sense of gratitude. Embracing distribution encourages us to adopt a mindset of stewardship, which can help balance our perspective on ownership. It also challenges the notion of acquiring possessions or people solely for the sake of power or status. By embracing a distributive approach, we acknowledge that true happiness is not found in material possessions but rather in our relationships with others.

It's crucial to prioritise distributive practices in regard to our economic beliefs and climate management. Our current patriarchal system's exploitation of people and resources only exacerbates the divide between those who have excess and those who have nothing. This moral issue also poses a significant danger, as history has shown societies can only tolerate so much imbalance before reacting, often violently. With our world's growing population and dwindling resources, continuing with patriarchal practices could lead us down a path of catastrophe. Adopting a more distributive and sharing ideology is essential to prevent this outcome.

Being Co-operative:

Cooperation is crucial for achieving common goals and building positive relationships in various contexts. Effective communication, mutual respect, and acknowledgement of each other's skills and expertise are essential components of cooperation. By working together towards common, sustainable, and beneficial goals, we can create a better world for all. Cooperation is a vital aspect of all relationships, personal, professional and social, and we as a species have evolved to work with each other in a cooperative manner.

Unfortunately, without realising it, we even cooperate with negative and harmful behaviours, both towards ourselves and towards others. This is the power of unconscious influence and how we often accept ways of thinking and acting without critical analysis. The risk of this happening is reduced by consciously choosing to cooperate in a democratic and distributive manner.

Once we open ourselves to the conscious choice to cooperate, either with our partner or in our work or social life, another crucial factor of cooperation becomes apparent: trust.

When individuals work together towards a common goal, they are more likely to build trust in each other's abilities and intentions. Trust allows for a more effective exchange of ideas and is essential for successful collaboration. In order for that trust to be built, we need to communicate effectively. Good communication involves mutual respect and an acknowledgment of each participant's value, skills and expertise. We can see this easily in our workplace, where cooperation can lead to increased productivity, or on the sports field, where teams that cooperate and work together are the most successful.

Cooperation does not replace the idea of competition but is conceptually of a higher ethical order. For example, in sports, a team learns to cooperate with one another before it becomes a competitive force on the playing field. Competition without sound values leads to things like doping, cheating, and commercial exploitation of the players and spectators. So in the context of sport, the player first agrees to co-operate with the sport's rules before they enter the competition. So, although the sport is an exemplar of the competitive spirit, it is also deeply embedded within a cooperative process.

One issue with competitiveness is that it has infiltrated areas where it is not appropriate. Engaging in competition solely for the sake of winning is a characteristic of patriarchy. In contrast, cooperation necessitates a shared and clearly defined goal or purpose that all parties have agreed upon. To embrace these values, we must exhibit empathy and let go of the patriarchal mask we have been conditioned to wear.

For example, in healthcare settings, patients are more likely to trust providers who work together seamlessly and communicate effectively, leading to better health outcomes.

Positive relationships are a key component of cooperation and cannot exist without mutual trust and respect. Building positive relationships requires effort and investment of time, but the benefits are numerous. Positive relationships can increase productivity, improve mental health, and improve overall well-being. According to a study published in the Journal of Social and Personal Relationships, positive relationships at work are associated with greater job satisfaction and lower levels of stress. In addition, according to a study by the Society for Human Resource Management, cooperation and teamwork are among the top skills employers look for in job candidates.

7

The Issue of Good & Great

Core Ideas to Being 'Great'.

"By a great man, however, we mean a man who, because of his spiritual gifts, his character, and other qualities, deserves to be called great and who, as a result, earns the power to influence others." – Fredrik Bajer.

Is a "New Masculinity" accompanied by a revised definition of greatness? I believe so, as the term has been overused and attributed to individuals who do not truly deserve such a title. Let's delve into Bajer's intriguing but vague quote. What does he mean by "spiritual gifts, character, and other qualities"? Additionally, Bajer mentions that great men have earned the ability to sway others. Overall, Bajer's definition leaves us with more questions than answers. I am sceptical that most men in history who have been known as 'great' have earned this power. They have been men who were able to dominate and demand control over others. When we think of men known as 'great', they are usually patriarchs. Some excelled in religious pursuits, while others stood out in politics or on the battlefield. Names like Pompey, Alexander, Frederick, and Peter are all associated with the label of 'great'. Bajer suggests these men possessed a spiritual gift or certain personality traits that led to their greatness. However, history tends to be written by the victors, not the masses or the defeated. Therefore, the label of 'greatness' is often self-awarded.

The subject of greatness becomes even more complex when we examine many 'great' men's personal and public lives. Why? Because many 'great' men had some serious character flaws. Some were powerful men, leading through fear, while others were highly persuasive yet lacked discipline in day-to-day actions, operating on a 'do as I say, not as I do' principle. Many struggled with addictions and other vices. Does that still qualify them to be called 'great'? You might argue that it's ok; they are only human. Being human implies being fallible or flawed, but to what degree?

Let's look at a few examples. An obvious choice, to begin with, is Alexander the Great, who exhibited fatal weaknesses: highly narcissistic, vicious cruelty, and infamous drinking. Then there were the Popes. A whole host of them did not live according to the ideals which they professed. In fact, they often lived their lives more aligned with the seven deadly sins than the Ten Commandments or the teachings of Jesus.

Similarly, amongst politicians, many 'great' political leaders were found by history to be cruel, ruthless, corrupt, and mostly self-interested, many pathologically so. Yet they led countries, corporations and institutions, and during their time in power, many were revered by those they led. Stalin is an example of a leader loved by many Russians, some of whom even today refuse to believe the truth about his misuse of power. The sheer breadth of the crimes he committed against his own people rivals the nightmare caused by Hitler and his cronies, who also drew vast, admiring crowds of adoring followers.

Let's take a look at some definitions of 'great' that are offered to us. In trawling the Internet, I came across a web page authored by Sean Russell that offered descriptions of thirty-four people who are considered great people. Now, I'm not going to go through all of them, but I will choose a couple. As always, I found it interesting that there are a couple of types of definitions, and they can be categorised.

Firstly, there are definitions of great that focus on Actions. These are, in my view, the more common ones, and they attribute greatness to taking the right actions, whether to achieve personal goals and/or social ones. John Romaniello, a Fitness Expert, focuses on the legacy of achieving great things. Chris Lee, a motivational speaker, says, "My definition of greatness is having my life, actions, and results align with my vision. To me, that's greatness."

Others define greatness based on Feelings. For Pat Flynn, greatness is about inspiration, and for Dr. Jeff Spencer, it is about honouring yourself. For others, it's about happiness. Then we have those who believe that social consciousness, being kind, sharing, inspiring others, and giving are the foundation of greatness.

What if the definition was a lot simpler? What if greatness could be defined by simply being and doing that which allows us to make a consistent, persistent and constructive change for the betterment of ourselves and others? One where we can empower ourselves and others to lead a great life?

What if a great man enables himself and others to flourish?

This leaves us with the question of what it means for a human being to flourish. One of ancient Greece's foremost philosophers, Aristotle, called human flourishing 'Eudaemonia'. Psychologist Carol Ryff has subsequently taken Aristotle's ideas further and developed a six-factor framework:

Autonomy. I have confidence in my opinions, even if they contradict the general consensus.

Environmental Mastery. In general, I feel I am in charge of the situation in which I live.

Personal Growth. Having new experiences that challenge how you think about yourself and the world is important.

Positive Relations with Others. People would describe me as giving and willing to share my time with others.

Purpose in Life. Some people wander aimlessly through life, but I am not one of them.

Self-Acceptance. I like most aspects of my personality.

My view is that we need to reorder this a little. First, we need to take care of our physical well-being and then work on our psychological resilience. We should then be actively engaged in social interactions and finally actualise ourselves in aligning this to a strong purpose that gives our existence meaning from which we can act with intention. Much like Maslow's hierarchy of needs, we ascend a pyramid with our physical needs at the bottom, supporting our psychological, social and spiritual needs.

Physical:

To have our identity focused completely on our physicality leaves us emotionally and psychologically vulnerable, not only to the consequences of accidents and injuries but to the ravages of time. Age becomes the enemy. As we age, we lose power and strength. We heal more slowly from injuries and are left with chronic complaints like arthritis. Ageing as a process is challenging at best, but those whose only sense of identity, purpose and self-esteem is located in their physical strength have nothing to fall back on when that is inevitably lost.

Physical strength was crucial in men's lives when most activities required it, and it remains important even in today's modern lifestyle. While a man's strength is a valuable asset, it shouldn't be the sole basis for his identity as a man. If it is, he may become one-dimensional and lack balance as a well-rounded human being.

As we age, our physical needs and capabilities change. It is important to maintain a balance between caring for our physical selves and other aspects of our lives. This includes getting enough rest, eating a well-balanced diet, staying active, and caring for health concerns. By prioritising our physical well-being, we can better focus on other aspects of our lives and be more productive and fulfilled. Remember, caring for ourselves is not selfish; it's necessary for our overall well-being.

In our early development, our focus is on achieving physical mastery. Children revel in learning how to master their bodies. As most of you know, our cultural norms about gender heavily influence this. As we grow, there will be distinct attitudinal boundaries layered on our experience, and they will be expressed through approval/disapproval and through the opportunities we are given to experiment and explore. All children will test themselves at every opportunity to get a sense of strength and coordination, and it will depend on whether a child has siblings or the opportunity to mix with other children as to how this occurs. For most of us, this will be done through a mix of solo play, like kicking a ball around the yard or climbing on things, and time spent with other children in parks or at social gatherings. As we get older, it may be in the context of a sport. This not only provides children with the physical benefits of being active but also psychological and social benefits.

By six months, a significant change occurs in how a human infant interacts with its world. They now have more physical control. They are able to sit up to reach for things that catch their attention, their eyes can now focus, and they have started to orient objects better in space, mainly towards the mouth. Physically, the baby's development is going ahead in leaps and bounds.

As we grow older, the physical differences between boys and girls become more apparent, along with the gender stereotypes that persist in our cultures. Boys tend to demonstrate their physical strength over girls, which can create challenges for both genders. The way children perceive and reflect on this depends on their upbringing. Boys are usually taught not to misuse their physical advantage. However, this coincides with boys and girls beginning to segregate into gender-specific groups during physical activities.

Physical development remains a crucial aspect of our well-being as we grow up and into adulthood, especially for men who focus on building their strength and size. Despite aging, we can continue to acquire and maintain new physical skills. However, our cultural and social conditioning affects how we view our physicality, and the patriarchal stereotypes target both genders, pressuring us to conform to a specific embodiment despite the genetic variations that naturally occur among humans.

This is the dark side to our understanding of our physicality. Patriarchy aligned men's physical strength with power in the context of its use to exert control over others. This, in turn, created divisions among men based on their size and strength. Within a patriarchal mindset, men have thought nothing of using their physical strength to take advantage of the ability it gives them to abuse those less physically endowed. The old adage that 'might is right' captures this, and historically, men have been significantly harmed, both psychologically and emotionally, by this misuse of physical power. Not only as victims of other men harassing, bullying, and assaulting them but as perpetrators against those who were, in turn, physically weaker than themselves, women.

Either individually or as tribes or nations, we have subjected ourselves and others to the ramifications of physical violence, and the toll on our shared humanity and the planet is only now being evaluated and patriarchy held to account.

At some point in our lives, regardless of who we are, we must accept the changes in our physical being and confront our mortality. The youthful feeling of invincibility must give way to a more thoughtful acceptance of reality. We are all susceptible to harm and death, and life is a precious gift that should not be taken for granted. We can choose to ignore this truth, fear to age, or use our mind to guide us through the changes and embrace our physical selves as part of our complete being.

This is about our body and what we do with it. I think this aspect revolves around four key functions to keep it nice and simple.

Sleep
Exercise
Relaxation

Nutrition.

Getting a good amount of quality sleep is crucial for our well-being and functioning.

In today's fast-paced society, many of us are overworked and overstimulated, making it difficult to get the recommended amount of sleep each night. However, getting enough sleep is essential for our physical and mental health. For example, studies have shown that lack of sleep can lead to a weakened immune system, increased risk of obesity, and even depression and anxiety. On the other hand, getting enough sleep can help improve memory, enhance creativity, and increase productivity.

There are a few other things that further add to our stress levels and, therefore, interfere with good sleep:

Alcohol and drugs, like speed and cocaine; prescription drugs like opioids; and coffee.

Overwork: working more than 9 hours a day can lead to serious sleep disturbance

Over-exercising

Excessive screen time, as in TV, computer time, smartphones and tablets.

Lack of good sleep hygiene, working in bed, watching TV in bed, taking your notebook and laptop to bed.

Likewise, engaging in physical activity isn't just an option; it's a prerequisite for maintaining a healthy body. Human beings are made to move, but our sedentary lifestyles require us to exercise or participate in sports to stay fit. It's encouraging to see more and more men recognising this and setting aside ample time for exercise. However, for some, it can turn into a competitive pursuit that causes more physical and psychological stress than is beneficial. Additionally, while exercise is important, it's not the same as relaxation. Another element of self-care that is often neglected is relaxation. This can take many forms, from meditation to taking a hot bath or simply taking a break from work to read a book or spend time with friends and family. Relaxation is important because it helps alleviate stress and anxiety, which can negatively impact our overall well-being. For instance, taking a few minutes to practice deep breathing exercises or meditating can help lower our heart rate and reduce feelings of tension and feeling overwhelmed.

In short, taking care of ourselves through proper sleep and relaxation practices is crucial for our physical and mental health. By prioritising these elements of self-care, we can improve our overall quality of life and feel more energised, focused, and resilient in the face of life's challenges.

It's crucial to remember that insufficient sleep, relaxation, and exercise can hinder the body's ability to handle our physical demands and the substances we consume. One of the main culprits behind this is cortisol, a hormone that increases during stress. Elevated cortisol levels can lead to various problems within the body, such as inflammation in the gut, which can impede nutrient absorption. Even if you maintain a healthy diet, if your cortisol levels remain high, your body will still be deprived of the necessary nutrients.

. So, let's ensure we care for ourselves in all aspects of our lives. To begin to thrive, we need to bring sleep, exercise, relaxation and nutrition into alignment.

Psychological:

William Shakespeare is widely remembered as an insightful playwright who used his work to offer his audience observations about the human condition. In his play 'Hamlet', he stated that our experiences are neither inherently good nor bad, but rather it is our perception and thoughts about these experiences that give them meaning. A significant portion of our emotional distress is a result of our thought patterns rather than external circumstances. This recognition highlights the importance of examining our thoughts clearly to manage our emotions, which is a core tenet of psychological well-being.

This requires reflection—thinking about our own thoughts, actions, and feelings. Ultimately, I must take responsibility for these aspects of myself to achieve emotional balance.

Assuming a high level of self-responsibility and accountability also entails the ability to respond appropriately to different situations. Essentially, it requires me to shed my robotic or habituated tendencies. So, how can I accomplish this?

Start with three simple steps:
1. Awareness: be aware of your thoughts
2. The feelings they generate
3. What they may be connected to

Often, our thoughts are mere observations that come and go without any conscious effort on our part. However, it is sometimes necessary to assess these thoughts and subject them to a litmus test of sorts, which involves assessing their logic, rationality, and objectivity. If a thought fails to meet one or more of these criteria, we must challenge them and re-examine how we are thinking.

It is important to note that stress can significantly impact our thought processes, causing us to become more negative, pessimistic, and catastrophic in our thinking. This, in turn, leads to increased feelings of distress and may even culminate in anxiety or depression.

When we refer to thinking, we are essentially talking about a range of cognitive processes, including beliefs, attitudes, values, and self-talk. It is crucial to pay attention to which of these processes is active at any given time.

Being Social:

In *Making Good Men Great: Surfing A New Masculinity,* the concept of 'Being Social' extends far beyond simple social interactions. It encapsulates a profound understanding of how our actions and behaviours integrate with the world at large, emphasising the ethical and moral dimensions of our engagement with others and society.

At the heart of 'Being Social' lies the critical evaluation of our motivations. Are our actions driven by unwavering integrity, or are they dictated by self-interest? This introspection demands an honest appraisal of whether we uphold values of honesty, fairness, and respect or primarily seek personal gain, potentially at others' expense.

Furthermore, 'Being Social' is deeply rooted in how we navigate our relationships. It's about fostering authentic connections, practising empathy, and engaging in meaningful and enriching interactions. These dynamics are pivotal in building supportive and understanding communities. Equally important is our role and contribution to society. This aspect challenges us to reflect on how our personal actions enhance social well-being, promoting values like equality, justice, and sustainability. It's a call to consider the broader implications of our behaviour.

Self-reflection on our social impact is also a cornerstone of this concept. It involves a continuous assessment and adjustment of our behaviours to ensure they are inclusive, responsible, and beneficial to the community at large.

Navigating social spaces within this new masculinity paradigm also means being acutely aware of social dynamics, power structures, and cultural norms. It's about understanding the influence of our identity and privileges on our interactions and taking active responsibility to address and rectify inequalities. Activism and advocacy form another crucial element of 'Being Social.' This involves taking a stand for justice, challenging oppressive systems, and utilising our voice and actions to drive positive social change.

Lastly, 'Being Social' encompasses the delicate balance between attending to personal needs and contributing to the collective good. This balance is vital in fostering a society that is both harmonious and equitable, reflecting the core principles of the "Making Good Men Great" initiative.

Being Spiritual:

When we think of the concept of spirituality, we tend to focus on the fundamental questions of life. Those that transcend the day-to-day realities of our lives, such as the existence of a god or a soul, or the origin of the Universe, and what existed before the Big Bang. Many people have dedicated their entire lives to pondering just one of these questions, and some of the answers they have come up with provide frameworks and guidelines within which many people live their lives. It's important to remember when we discuss spirituality that in our society, religion and other esoteric beliefs are considered private matters, and we should not impose those beliefs on others and their choices.

However, spirituality can also be a means of introspection and reflection on one's own journey. It is an attitude of transcendence beyond the pragmatic and routine, a way to look at the 'BIG QUESTIONS' in one's own life. Some of us would use the concept of personal philosophy to describe the way we consider these questions.

1. Do you have a sense of purpose
2. that gives meaning to your life and
3. formulates your intentions for your actions?

Have you considered defining your purpose and how it could impact your life? Would it alter how you live, who you associate with, or what you do for a living? Spirituality plays a role in everyone's life, whether they realise it or not, as we all give meaning to our actions based on our beliefs and values. Ultimately, these beliefs and values shape our behaviour.

Alignment and Personal Evolution:

I am fortunate to reside in a delightful suburb that allows me to take lovely walks along some of the world's finest beaches. A golf course runs alongside the closest beach, and during a recent stroll, I observed a man preparing to tee off. He closed his eyes and allowed the club to swing through without striking the ball, a mental rehearsal technique commonly used in sports. Although I am not a golfer, I could tell from the club head's connection with the ball on his next swing that it was an exquisite stroke. The ball left the tee with a resounding crack reverberating throughout the golf course, flying straight onto the green. The most significant aspect was the ease with which the stroke was executed. The man smiled, and his friend gave him an approving nod and a friendly pat on the back. Our golfer demonstrated a critical component of playing sports: the concept of flow.

Mihaly Csikszentmihalyi[1975,1990] defined flow as a psychological state that can be achieved when the challenges and the skills in a situation are both high, This state occurs when an individual surpasses their average experience of challenge and skill in a given situation. Flow has intrigued athletes and performers alike, but it also applies to daily life. Eastern philosophies, particularly Buddhism, encourage practitioners to strive for a state of flow as much as possible, alongside awareness, alignment, and attunement, as it is crucial to living consciously. It is essential to consider flow as one of our primary objectives in our plan to thrive and not just survive.

Here are three steps to achieve a state of flow.

Step 1: Awareness

"After ten years of apprenticeship, Tenno achieved the rank of Zen teacher. One rainy day, he went to visit the famous master Nan-in. When he walked in, the master greeted him with a question, "Did you leave your wooden clogs and umbrella on the porch?" "Yes," Tenno replied. "Tell me," the master continued, "did you place your umbrella to the left of your shoes or to the right? Tenno did not know the answer and realised he had not yet attained full awareness. So he became Nan-in's apprentice and studied under him for ten more years."

As a therapist, I encourage men to broaden their awareness into three critical zones: the inner, middle, and outer zones.

These zones are highlighted in Gestalt therapy, a form of psychotherapy that emphasises personal responsibility and focuses on the individual's experience in the present moment, the therapeutic process, and the environment. These zones are crucial for understanding how individuals perceive and interact with their environment and themselves. Each zone represents different aspects of an individual's awareness and contributes to their overall perception and experience of the world.

1. Inner Zone: This zone of awareness pertains to sensations and experiences that occur within the body. It includes an individual's internal physiological sensations, emotions, and thoughts. The Inner Zone is where one becomes aware of one's feelings, needs, and bodily sensations, such as hunger, tension, or relaxation. In Gestalt therapy, bringing awareness to this zone can help clients become more attuned to their authentic selves and their immediate needs and feelings. It encourages individuals to notice and accept their internal experiences without judgment, fostering a deeper understanding of themselves.

2. Middle Zone: The Middle Zone relates to the awareness of one's presence in and interaction with the social world, including relationships with others. It encompasses how individuals perceive their roles, interactions, and the dynamics within their interpersonal relationships. This zone highlights the importance of understanding our own impact on others and how others affect us as individuals. Gestalt therapy uses this awareness to explore and improve interpersonal relationships, communication, and the capacity for intimacy and connection. It aims to help individuals recognise and address patterns in relationships that may be unproductive or harmful.

3. Outer Zone: The Outer Zone involves awareness of the environment and the broader context in which we as individuals live. This includes the physical space around us, cultural norms, social expectations, and other external factors that influence our experience and behaviour. In Gestalt therapy, awareness of the Outer Zone helps clients understand how their environment affects them and how they can interact more effectively with it. It encourages a mindful engagement with the world and an acknowledgment of the influence of external factors on our lives.

Gestalt therapy emphasises the fluidity between these zones and the importance of integrating awareness across them. By becoming more aware of each zone and how they interrelate, individuals can achieve a more holistic understanding of themselves and their place in the world. This comprehensive awareness is seen as a path toward greater self-support, autonomy, and authenticity, leading to more fulfilling and meaningful lives.

Expanding awareness in these three zones can positively change our lives. To achieve this, I urge my clients to focus on three key areas: self-awareness, interpersonal awareness, and situational awareness. Self-awareness involves becoming more mindful of our thoughts, emotions, and behaviours. Interpersonal awareness involves becoming more aware of our interactions with others, leading to stronger relationships, better communication, and fewer conflicts. Situational awareness involves becoming more aware of our surroundings and context, leading to better decision-making and more effective responses to challenges and opportunities.

Like Tenno in the story, we must all work towards attaining full awareness to achieve our goals and find true fulfilment in life. By expanding our awareness into these three zones, we can better understand ourselves and the world around us and make positive changes that lead to greater happiness and success.

In our culture, much of our time is spent in the middle zone, especially if you are a male. We are trained to value reason above all else. Being logical and rational is useful but less so in the absence of other information, especially that of the senses and, importantly our inner zone, our emotions.

Step 2: Alignment - what is it?

Most dictionaries define alignment in the following way:

Alignment:

Arrangement or position in a straight line or in parallel lines.

The process of adjusting parts so that they are in proper relative position: The condition of having parts so adjusted:

A ground plan: Blueprints for the building included an alignment and a profile.

The act of aligning or the condition of being aligned.

An arrangement or alliance of groups: a new alignment of factions in the party.

In Sports:

An arrangement or positioning of players: a defensive alignment.

The grouping or positioning of teams, as in a conference or league.

Put simply, alignment refers to adjusting or arranging something in a straight line or in the correct position. It can also refer to agreeing or matching with something else.

After going through various types of psychological literature, it is evident that there is a limited focus on and explanation of the topic of alignment. Despite being used in multiple fields and gaining some popularity, it is not given much attention. Hence, what exactly does alignment mean? In human wellness terms, alignment is the integration or harmonisation of our physiology, psychological make-up, values, and relationship with ourselves and others. In other words, I am aligning my zones of awareness. In alignment, we are in a state of well-being. Through that process, we begin to thrive or, in Aristotle's words, flourish.

Misalignments create tension. We are in disharmony. Feelings of distress, insecurity and anxiety emerge, and we cannot experience any flow. Things will be more stressful and less fulfilling, and they are often frustrated with conflicts.

Regarding relationships, it's crucial to connect with our partner, our children, and all of those who are significant in our lives. This connection involves sharing our values, aspirations, and goals and working towards them together in harmony as we navigate life's journey.

Our careers and vocations are about aligning the vision, values, culture and results we are trying to achieve collectively.

Step 3: Attunement

Attunement is the ability to understand and respond to another person's emotional needs and mood. To connect with someone, attunement is essential. An individual who is well-attuned can react appropriately by using language and behaviour that aligns with the other person's emotional state. They can accurately identify emotions and moods in others and adjust their own response accordingly. When it comes to parenting, attuned parents can better recognise their children's needs and provide appropriate support. Although most parents want their children to thrive and lead fulfilling lives, research suggests that parents must lead by example for their children to achieve similar success. Merely communicating verbally is not enough to guide children towards happiness and fulfilment.

I believe that awareness, alignment, and attunement create flow. When I began to rethink what it means to be a man in the 21st century, I realised that one of the primary issues is that most men are not in flow. We automatically participate unconsciously in patterns of behaviour from which we expect different returns. As Einstein put it, that is insane.

Granted, change is not easy, but the payoff is worth it. It will:

1. Improve our relationship with ourselves,
2. Improve our relationship with 'others'. That includes partners, children, friends, and colleagues,
3. and it improves our degree of constructive influence on other men.

So, essentially:

flow = awareness + alignment + attunement

Now the question is, what, as an individual, do I need to align?

8

The Next Phase of Our Evolution

Throughout our lives, we experience continuous evolution. As men, it's important to ask ourselves various questions to aid in our personal growth. With changing times come different expectations and roles. However, we may wonder how to identify aspects of ourselves that require improvement and a fresh perspective. We may also question how to initiate this self-assessment and track our progress.

For us as men, I believe there is a developmental process that we need to be aware of, acknowledge and work with. In most traditional societies, certain rites were established to achieve exactly that. These rites generally took us through four realms of being; the physical, the fullness of reason, [mindful], authenticity, and finally being soulful, that place where we have learnt to temper ourselves with wisdom. These rites of passage were believed to bring us in touch with an 'other' realm, a spiritual place where we would be more connected to the whole, whether you call it God, the All, Dreamtime or the Great Spirit. Those performing the rites and those undergoing them were bound together and to the wholeness of the collective.

The time chosen for these rites was aligned with the physical changes that heralded the transition from child to man. Just as girls turned into women through the flow of blood, many of these rites for men included some form of bloodletting. However, as we moved further into a settled and agricultural lifestyle, transitioning from boy to man became a part of joining the productive workforce or the military or clergy. For most of the last few thousand years, this still occurred around puberty; however, in today's world, boys are not expected to take their place as men until they are much older. Sometimes, they are in their mid to late twenties if they have pursued long courses of formal education.

Now in the post-industrial world, the recognition of the journey through life's stages and the learning accompanying it, has been replaced by a mechanistic view of being human. We struggle to define aspects of ourselves, such as consciousness, intuition, and transpersonal experience. In order to remedy this, we need to raise our awareness of these three critical spheres in our evolution.

Now, let me walk you briefly through each phase. In each stage, we use awareness, alignment and attunement.

Being Mindful:

In *Making Good Men Great: Surfing A New Masculinity*, the concept of 'Being Mindful' is dissected into two interrelated yet distinct interpretations, both essential in the journey towards a more evolved, introspective, and conscious form of masculinity.

First Interpretation: <u>Understanding and Mastering the Mind</u>

Beyond Cognitive Processing: In this context, the mind is more than just an organ for processing data. It is not just computational. Furthermore, it embodies our consciousness. It's the interplay between our brain's physical workings and conscious experiences. Understanding the mind involves recognising its capabilities beyond logical and rational processing.

Evolution of Mental Capacities: Our mental faculties, such as self-reflection, reasoning, and empathy, evolve over time. They are not innate but develop through stimulation and experience. The mind's ability to process, learn, memorise, and communicate information has been crucial in human evolution.

Discipline and Self-Awareness: Mastering the mind requires discipline to regulate thoughts rationally and objectively. This involves developing self-awareness, critical reflection, and mental resilience. Cognitive, behavioural, and emotional flexibility are key components in this mastery.

Separation of Thoughts and Emotions: An essential aspect is the capacity to observe our thoughts as distinct from our emotions. This differentiation allows for rational reflection and more effective decision-making.

Influence of Relationships and Experiences: Our relationships and experiences heavily influence who we become. These interactions shape critical reflection, a skill evolving from self-awareness and communication.

Mind Mastery as a Double-Edged Sword: While mastering the mind is crucial, there's a caution against becoming too intellectualised or overly reasonable at the expense of emotional expression and vulnerability.

Second Interpretation: <u>Mindfulness as Proposed by Bishop Lau (2004)</u>

Self-Regulation of Attention: This involves maintaining attention on immediate experiences and facilitating increased awareness of mental events in the present moment.

Orientation Towards Experiences: Adopting an attitude of curiosity, openness, and acceptance towards one's experiences in the present moment. This means being intentionally attentive to thoughts, feelings, and sensations without judgment.

Integrating Both Interpretations:

To be truly mindful in the context of *Making Good Men Great: Surfing A New Masculinity*, one must exercise both interpretations. This means having both a disciplined, self-aware mastery of the mind and an open, accepting approach to present experiences.

Practical Application: Mindfulness is not just a theoretical concept but is often practised in everyday life, sometimes without conscious realisation. It involves being present in the moment, whether in personal reflection, interaction with others, or even in mundane tasks.

Secure and Satisfying State of Mind: By integrating both interpretations of mindfulness, men can achieve a state of mind that is both secure and satisfying, enhancing their overall well-being and ability to engage thoughtfully and intentionally in various aspects of their lives.

In the new masculinity framework, ' being mindful' means cultivating a deep understanding of the mind's potential and embracing a present-oriented, accepting approach to experiences. This holistic view of mindfulness is fundamental in the journey towards a more reflective, conscious, and fulfilling form of masculinity.

This is a brief mindfulness exercise of five or six breaths to be practised several times per day, anywhere and at any time.

1. Stop and become aware of what you are doing right now, where you are and what you are thinking
2. Become aware of your breathing for about a minute or half a dozen breaths.
3. Expand your awareness to your whole body and then to your environment.

Take a very definite posture ... relaxed, back erect, but not stiff, letting your body express a sense of being present and awake.

Close your eyes. Becoming aware of what is going through your mind; what thoughts are around? Here, again, as best you can, note the thoughts as mental events.... Note them, and then we note the feelings that are around at the moment ... in particular, turning toward any sense of discomfort or unpleasant feelings. So rather than try to push them away or shut them out, acknowledge them, perhaps say them out loud. And similarly with sensations in the body... Are there sensations of tension, of holding? And again, be aware of them, simply noting them. OK, that's how it is right now.

The second step is to collect your awareness by focusing on a single object—the movements of the breath. So now you really gather yourself, focus your attention down there in the movements of your abdomen or other breath focus point such as the nostrils or roof of the mouth, the rise and fall of the breath ... spending a minute or so to focus on the movement of the abdominal wall ... moment by moment, breath by breath, as best we can. So that you know when the breath is moving in, and you know when the breath is moving out. Just bind your awareness to the movement pattern down there ... gathering yourself, using the anchor of the breath to really be present.

And now, as a third step, having gathered yourself to some extent, you allow your awareness to expand. As well as being aware of the breath, we also include a sense of the body as a whole. So that we get this more spacious awareness... A sense of the body as a whole, including any tightness or sensations related to holding in the shoulders, neck, back, or face ... following the breath as if your whole body is breathing and holding it all in this slightly softer ... more spacious awareness.

And then, when you are ready, allow your eyes to open and mindfully continue with your daily activity.

Being Authentic:

In the transformative journey towards Making Good Men Great: Surfing A New Masculinity, the principle of 'Being Authentic' emerges as a cornerstone. Authenticity in this context is a multifaceted concept that encompasses self-expression, emotional awareness, vulnerability, and integrity. It is about embodying one's true self, unshackled by social pressures or traditional gender norms. Let's delve deeper into the various dimensions of this principle:

Self-Expression and Integrity: Authenticity involves expressing oneself respectfully and assertively, aligning actions and words with one's values and beliefs. It's about having the courage to stand by one's convictions, even when they go against the grain. This kind of integrity fosters a life that is congruent with one's true self, as opposed to a life shaped by external expectations or social norms.

Embracing Vulnerability: A key aspect of being authentic is allowing oneself to be vulnerable. This means openly expressing a range of emotions, including those that are often suppressed in traditional masculinity, such as sadness, fear, or hurt. Vulnerability is not a weakness but a strength that signifies emotional maturity and self-awareness. It allows for deeper connections with others and a more fulfilling emotional life.

Overcoming Defence Mechanisms: Authenticity requires moving away from aggressive or defensive behaviours often used to mask vulnerability. Recognising and abandoning these mechanisms is essential in cultivating a more honest and open way of being.

Self-Assurance and Emotional Security: Understanding and being comfortable with one's identity and character fosters emotional courage. An emotionally secure man can make decisions aligned with his values, benefiting not only himself but also those around him. This self-assuredness is fundamental to achieving eudaemonia, a state of being that is characterised by fulfilment and happiness.

Constructive Engagement and Conflict Management: Living authentically equips a man to be responsive rather than reactive. This approach enhances the ability to listen actively, engage in meaningful dialogues, and manage conflicts constructively. It involves recognising negative tactics like contempt, blame, and criticism as harmful and choosing instead to engage in positive, respectful communication.

Independence from External Approval: An authentic man does not seek validation from others for his choices or actions. This independence from external approval signifies a strong sense of self and contributes to the ability to live a life that is true to one's values and beliefs.

In summary, 'Being Authentic' in the context of 'Making Good Men Great: A New Masculinity' is about embracing one's true self, with all its vulnerabilities and strengths. It involves a commitment to living with integrity, emotional openness, and a deep understanding of one's values and beliefs. This authentic way of living allows men to forge genuine relationships, make values-aligned decisions, and ultimately lead a life of purpose and fulfilment.

Being Soulful:

In the framework of *Making Good Men Great: Surfing A New Masculinity*, the concept of 'Being Soulful' represents a transformative stage in the evolution of masculinity. This stage transcends mere intellectual understanding and embodies a deeper, more holistic form of wisdom. Being soulful is about integrating knowledge with empathy, introspection, and a profound sense of purpose. It is a shift from acquiring information to living by the wisdom gleaned from experiences, relationships, and self-awareness.

From Knowledge to Wisdom: In this paradigm, knowledge is not just accumulated but is transformed into wisdom. This transformation occurs through reflection, life experiences, and the willingness to learn not only from success but also from failure. Wisdom here is seen as the ability to apply knowledge in ways that are compassionate, empathic, and for the greater good.

Spiritual Engagement: Being soulful in the context of a new masculinity involves a spiritual alignment that goes beyond traditional religious practices. It is about connecting with something greater than oneself, whether that's through nature, meditation, art, or community. This spiritual engagement fosters a deeper understanding of oneself and one's place in the world.

Beyond the Adolescent Ego: This stage involves transcending the adolescent ego, which is often competitive and focused on personal gain. Being soulful means moving towards a more mature perspective that values collaboration, empathy, and understanding. It's about recognising that one's actions have consequences beyond the self and do affect the larger community.

Conscious Legacy and Social Impact: At this stage, men are acutely aware of the legacy they are creating and the impact of their actions on future generations. This consciousness drives them to act responsibly and ethically, not just in personal matters but in their broader social and environmental impact. They understand that true masculinity involves nurturing, protecting, and contributing positively to society.

Integrated Existence: Being soulful signifies a harmonious integration of all aspects of one's life. It's about aligning one's actions with core values, leading to a congruent and authentic existence. This integrated approach breaks down the compartmentalisation often seen in traditional masculinity, where emotional, spiritual, and relational aspects are kept separate from other areas of life.

'Being Soulful' within the context of 'Making Good Men Great: A New Masculinity' is about evolving into a state of being where knowledge, emotional depth, spiritual awareness, a deep sense of connection and a sense of responsibility towards the future are seamlessly integrated. It represents a holistic, mature, and reflective form of masculinity that contributes positively to individual growth and the betterment of society.

9

Men and Relationships

Rejecting Narcissism

'The eternal question 'Who am I' must be weighed against an even deeper question: 'Who are we?' We are writing each other's stories as much as our own. (Mackay, Hugh, 2015)

Patriarchy wants us to be territorial, hierarchical, acquisitional, and competitive. In the book's first section, I argued strongly that this paradigm of manhood no longer works. It doesn't work because it fosters narcissistic men who are trained to act like it's 'all about me.' This attitude makes intimate and functional relationships not just difficult but virtually impossible.

It is by no means a coincidence that narcissism has become an epidemic in the population at a time when our institutions, corporations, and political agendas are almost entirely focused on an economic ideology driven by acquisition and competitiveness. This is clearly reflected in the leadership styles and lack of ethics among many politicians and corporate leaders.

Now, some might argue that being selfish is a good thing. It has given many the focus and drive to achieve a high level of success, with all of the money and power that goes with that success. So, before we go any further, I would like to remind you that the notion that success revolves around money and power is an essentially patriarchal ideal. And most importantly, selfishness and narcissism require that you disconnect yourself from any moral considerations and adopt a purely instrumental perspective. Narcissism comes at a price. Individually, it makes us more vulnerable to stress and being emotionally disturbed and costs us our relationships. So, in the long-term, being narcissistic is not a good thing, no matter how much wealth and power you accumulate.

Collectively, narcissism impoverishes society because it instrumentalises relationships within the community. Relationships only have value if there is something in it for me. It also trivialises the projects that enhance our humanity and connectedness. Given that human society depends on cooperation, which is the very reason we formed societies for our mutual survival, the increase in general narcissism does not bode well for our future.

Empathy:

The counterpoint to narcissism is a good dose of empathy. Any discussion examining the issue of masculinity that does not include a reflection on the importance of empathy in the evolution of men is missing the point. So the burning question is, how can we help men increase their emotional awareness and range and their ability to empathise with others? An increasing emphasis has been placed on educating young children to be more emphatic because we frequently make the assumption that adults cannot increase their capacity to develop empathy; you've either got it or you don't. Not true. Research has repeatedly shown that empathy can be taught and enhanced throughout our lives.

So, where to start? Roman Krznaric, the author of "Empathy: Why it Matters and How to Get It." talks about the six habits of Highly Emphatic People (HEP). He suggests that by deliberately focusing on these habits and putting them into your everyday life, you will increase your level of empathy. This is not a new idea. Aristotle argued that to build a good character, we needed to practice being good, to become habituated to acting in a way that was in accord with who we wanted to be.

Habit 1: Cultivate curiosity about strangers

Habit 2: Challenge prejudices and discover commonalities.

Habit 3: Try another person's life.

Habit 4: Listen hard and open up.

Habit 5: Inspire mass action and social change

Habit 6: Develop an ambitious imagination.

Developing the habits of curiosity, open-mindedness, and active listening can greatly improve your life. By cultivating these habits, you will gain a deeper understanding of others and their experiences while becoming more in touch with your thoughts and feelings. It takes around 30 days to form a habit, so practising these habits intentionally until they become second nature is necessary. As you build closer connections with those around you, including both close friends and acquaintances, you'll find that bigger-picture habits, such as imagination and sparking positive change, will naturally follow.

Once you become comfortable with these new ways of being in the world, the next step would be to:

Teach your children by modelling what you are focused on.

Talk to them about empathy.

Help them put it into practice.

Bring it into your community by talking about it.

Take it into your workplace and make it part of your values set.

Another key attitude that sits next to and reinforces empathy is kindness. Being kind to yourself and others enables you to let go of automatic judgments and critiques that undermine empathy. Being able to be considerate of another person's situation is a first step to being able to empathise with them. The key to remember is that we must evolve beyond these inflexible and restrictive ideas of traditional masculinity that patriarchy has moulded us into being. This outmoded approach to masculinity is intolerant of anyone who is in any way different from the promoted stereotype. The level of anxiety we experience when we challenge the demands of the stereotype is the truth-telling feature of how strong the patriarchal imperative is in our psyche.

A good example of this is what happens if you suggest to most men that they stop 'doing'. They get agitated having to face 'not doing' because traditionally, doing actions are valued as more important than simply 'being' or focusing on relationships, including their relationship with themselves. By constantly distracting themselves from their emotional states, men are able to continue to focus on tasks that they have been trained to think are important without feeling guilty. It essentially stops men from reflecting inward.

The fact is that relationships, whether with one's self or others, require the ability to be engaged in the moment, to be aware of yourself and those around you, and to be attuned to yourself as well as them. In order to understand another's point of view, you need to be able to put yourself in their place, to empathise with what they are experiencing. This is necessary for true attachment and the emotional fulfilment that this brings. If we don't attend to those around us, they will gradually disconnect from us. Often, this will take the form of conflict and cause distress for everyone involved. We have all seen this, and many of us have experienced it. I recently watched a father and his daughter, who is about nine years old, negotiate the challenge of arriving at the beach with all the gear and paraphernalia that goes with a summer's day at the ocean. As the Dad unloaded the car, a phone call interrupted said activity. Instantly, I sensed a great deal of irritation in the girl. With a deep sigh, she started to take over, unpacking the car and piling stuff on the footpath. Having emptied the boot, she sat down on a beach chair and waited. Unfortunately, Dad took this as a signal to keep talking on the phone. Several minutes passed. Suddenly, the girl bursts out, 'Dad, get off the phone!' Dad held up his hand and said, 'In a minute.' She responded in a flash with, 'You always say that!'

This was an opportunity for connection and enjoyment of time together that was lost to both of them by this guy prioritising a phone call. His inattention signalled his valuing of whomever he was talking to over his child, at least in that girl's eyes. Now, he would probably be shocked to realise this, but this is the reality of how we emotionally react. He displayed no empathy for her feeling of being abandoned for a phone call, and her response tells you that he does this all the time.

It doesn't take too much imagination to figure out that her experience of the day has been spoiled. She will probably react to this by being difficult, possibly surly, possibly openly hostile.

She is the child. It is not her responsibility to work at making sure that the connection between herself and her father is strong and loving. I have no doubt that this guy loves his daughter, but his actions do not tell her that, and the old adage 'actions speak louder than words' is absolutely true. What we do and DON'T do is just as powerful as communication as what we say and what we DON'T say. It is interpreted by others, filtered through their experiences of you and your previous actions, and inspires emotional reactions. Over time, these emotional reactions form the basis for beliefs about what is true about the relationship.

We don't have to look far to find someone we know or know of who has become depressed because they have suffered a physical injury. It's the same for those injuries you can't see, which people don't discuss. Not feeling loved, accepted or connected can lead to a cascade of physical, psychological or social problems. It is in our relationships, and in the pursuit of goals that inspire us that we find a sense of belonging.

Relationships are reciprocal and a two-way street. They need tending and nurturing, so alongside the practical responsibilities we might have in our lives, we have responsibilities within our relationships. These are often much harder and more complex than any other area of our lives. To do this well, we must have a good idea of what a good relationship feels like. The place to start is by forming a good relationship with ourselves; to do this, we need self-awareness.

In order to enhance our self-awareness, the easiest place to start is to look inward to your sense of who you are and ask: What do I value? What characteristics of being human are worthwhile cultivating, and have I done that so far in my life? This question encompasses all areas of our lives, and it can lead to some very significant self-reflection. Whatever you believe is a good way to act in the world usually rests on your values and your idea of yourself as a person. This is where many of us will find that we hold automatic and unconscious ideas about ourselves as men that we are now questioning. This may lead to a rethinking of those ideas, a refining of those values you wish to hold onto, and those you no longer ascribe to. Becoming aware of yourself so that you are thinking, feeling and acting in a way that is aligned with the values you embrace helps you feel confident that you are the person you want to be. This is the person who is having a relationship with the other people in your life. In the context of your relationship with your children, this is the person they get to know as they grow up in your care.

Relationships take time to develop and need you to be available physically and emotionally. You need to be present. Many men feel pressured by time constraints. There are multiple and often competing demands on their time, all important or seemingly so. How do you juggle these demands so that you have the time you need to spend with your family and friends? How do you ensure that you are not only physically present but also emotionally and psychologically present? How do you align the way you make choices about using your time with your intentions and aspirations as a man? What expectations do other people have of you?

At the heart of human well-being are relationships. We are social beings. Hence Hugh Mackay's quote. 'We are writing each other's stories as much as our own'. Whenever I speak of the need for men to initiate the conversation on rethinking masculinity, a few always challenge me that the media focuses too much on those few men who do the wrong thing. Those men that use violence against women, that rape, that exploit others. 'Most of us are not like that,' they argue vehemently. And I agree. Most men do not commit those atrocities. But many also do not speak out. They do not challenge other men when they express sexist, racist or any other discriminatory remarks. Remember: 'Evil happens when good men do nothing.' Good men challenge evil. Great men work to change the attitudes wherein evil might flourish.

The challenge for us as men is to be aware of how we conduct ourselves in our relationships with our partners, how we reach out to our sons and daughters, and what we do in the contexts of our communities. Someone in one of my men's groups observed that he was so unaware of how subtle and insidious patriarchal behaviour is in men, especially young men, that he had never really reflected on how men's behaviour in groups can quickly deteriorate into misogynistic behaviour. Suddenly, now, he can see it all around him.

10

Humans are Relational

Margaret Thatcher's infamous statement, "There is no such thing as society," reflects a particular understanding of human interactions and social obligations, emphasising individualism and personal responsibility. This statement reflects the ideology shaped by Ayn Rand and the philosophical underpinnings of neoliberalism. Rand's emphasis on individualism and rejection of collectivism significantly influenced Thatcher's, Reagan's, and most Western economists' views, as well as their influence on political and economic policies prioritising free-market capitalism and deregulation.

However, this is contrary to the scientific evidence gathered in the last forty years by neuroscientists such as Dr Mark Williams. In his most recent book 'Connected Species [2024], this distinguished cognitive neuroscientist has articulated clearly that this prioritising of the individual is one of the most harmful aspects of the patriarchal system and how it has influenced our perception and understanding of ourselves as individuals. The patriarchal concept of individualism characterises humans as abstract and detached from others, thus creating a sense of separateness. This has resulted in men being taught to be independent and self-sufficient at the expense of their emotional selves. The idea of standing alone and being "your own man" has been glorified, while the importance of emotional connections and vulnerability has been dismissed. This harmful perspective has created a society that values detachment and individual achievement over empathy and connection. Recognising this distorted view of individualism is crucial when working towards a more integrated and holistic approach that values emotional intelligence and interpersonal relationships.

This distorted view of humans as completely separate and abstract meant that women did not fit into the characterisation of an individual. As we have discussed earlier, within the patriarchal ideology, women were inferior and relegated to the home and the care of children. Their attachment, physical connection, and care of others were believed to diminish their capacity for individuality. Throughout history, this belief has divided society into public and private realms of life, with the public world of individual 'rational' men being valued more highly than the private world of 'emotional' women. This division was made possible by adding value to the tasks traditionally associated with men while dismissing the tasks of the private realm as less valuable.

This social division was reinforced by the traditional belief in biological determinism that dictated the gender stereotypes that locked both men and women into particular roles in society. Not only has this belief that women are only fit for the purpose of the care of others had a profound impact on women, it alienated men from their emotional lives. Men are considered biologically unfit for caring emotionally and practically for others. We have all been inculcated with the mantra that 'men are rational, and women are emotional'.

Because of this patriarchal ideology, women have been historically excluded from the public sphere and forced to be economically dependent on men. And men have been excluded from family life outside of the role of provider and authoritarian disciplinarian.

Another facet of this characterisation is that it fails to account for the situational reality of men's lives. The abstract, separate individual is thus alienated from their own context. Their family, socioeconomic position and class, all of the social realities of their lives are ignored, and they are launched into society to compete with each other for status, wealth and power. This denial of systemic inequalities and disadvantages exacerbates those differences, particularly for marginalised groups. Ultimately, a more nuanced approach that considers the complex ways in which social categorisations intersect is necessary for creating a fair and just society.

To illustrate the concept of intersectionality, let's consider the experiences of a black woman from a working-class background. This individual may face discrimination based on her race, gender, and socio-economic status, all at the same time. For instance, she may be more likely to experience racial profiling and police brutality due to her skin colour. At the same time, she may also face gender-based discrimination, such as the gender pay gap, and socio-economic disadvantages, such as limited access to quality education and healthcare.

Thus, Thatcher's statement fails to acknowledge the complex and interconnected nature of social issues. We need to recognise and address the intersections of various social categorisations if we want to create a fair and equal society for all.

Patriarchy is not about fairness and equality. An intersectional understanding of society highlights how individual identities are not just personal but shaped and influenced by broader social, political, and economic structures (Crenshaw, 1989). These structures can privilege certain groups (e.g., through legacy admissions to universities, wealth inheritance) while systematically disadvantaging others (e.g., through discriminatory policies and biases in legal and educational systems).

This view can also overlook the effects of systemic abuses on individuals and communities, such as those resulting from racial or economic discrimination. These forms of systemic abuse can have profound and long-lasting impacts, including psychological trauma, limited access to resources and opportunities, and a cycle of poverty and disadvantage.

Despite these challenges, our society has made significant strides in breaking down gender barriers and achieving greater equality. Women have entered the workforce in larger numbers, and their contributions to society are increasingly recognised and valued. Men are now more confident to participate in emotional and caring responsibilities. However, there is still much work to be done. Women still carry the burden of the majority of unpaid domestic work. To address this inequality and ensure that women are fully empowered and able to achieve true separateness from their traditional roles as caregivers and homemakers, we need to recognise and address the systemic barriers that prevent us from creating a more just and equal society for all.

A major problem we face in society is the way our conditioning has eroded the feminist goal of achieving equality in the recognition of all human life's endeavours. The workplace is still given more importance than the home, and success is only measured by professional achievements. The roles of raising children, managing the home, and providing care for others are undervalued compared to the work of paid employees. If we calculate the cost of outsourcing all of the tasks of managing a household and caring for children and another family to a paid worker, it becomes glaringly obvious that this work is economically valuable. We have attached value only to an individual's earnings, thereby devaluing those who do not earn a wage and the contribution they make to society.

This means that attempts by both men and women to try and change the workplace to be one that is more friendly to family and community have been continually hampered by the entrenched patriarchy of our institutions. It is still enormously difficult for men to take paternity leave without being seen as less devoted to their jobs than they 'should' be. The options for part-time work in some industries do not exist, and men who take time out to be the main caregivers of their children are judged as being 'different types of men', but not necessarily in a good way. The belief in ourselves as separate individuals, able to fend for ourselves and not needing anyone else, continues to be a powerful message in our society.

The fact is that "human beings have succeeded as the most dominant species on earth in large part due to our need to connect and cooperate"[Williams, 2024]. In fact, we would not have survived if we had not cooperated with each other. It was our ability to socialise and connect that catapulted our species to phenomenal heights of innovation through collaboration and specialisation. This drive has fine-tuned our unconscious perception of faces, facial expressions, body language, and touch. Our primitive drive to connect changes how we perceive the world and the people around us. We see, hear, empathise with, and understand others differently depending on whether they are a member of our in-group or not. This unconscious drive to connect can draw us together, but it also emphasises the differences between groups. Unfortunately, this wariness of difference is getting worse as overcrowding, technology, and the media often focus on our differences. We become more and more divided into groups as a result."

The profound impact of early relationships on our development underscores the fundamental human need for connection and the pivotal role of emotional intelligence in navigating these connections throughout life. Emotional intelligence, a concept popularised by Daniel Goleman, refers to the ability to recognise, understand, manage, and use our emotions positively to communicate effectively, empathise with others, overcome challenges, and defuse conflict. This capacity is deeply intertwined with the quality of our earliest attachments and continues to be shaped by our interactions and relationships.

The Role of Connection in Emotional Development:

From the moment of birth, the quality of our relationships with caregivers sets the foundation for our emotional landscape. Secure attachments foster a sense of safety and trust in the world, enabling us to explore our environments and relationships confidently. This security is the bedrock upon which emotional intelligence is built, as it allows for developing critical emotional skills, such as empathy, self-regulation, and the ability to understand and communicate one's feelings.

Emotional Intelligence and Relationships:

As we journey through life and interact with others, it becomes crucial to develop emotional intelligence – a set of skills that enable us to understand and manage our own emotions and those of others. Emotional intelligence allows us to empathise with others, putting ourselves in their shoes and responding compassionately. It also helps us communicate effectively, expressing our needs and concerns without escalating conflicts. Additionally, emotional intelligence equips us with strategies for managing conflicts in a healthy, constructive manner, ensuring that relationships are strengthened rather than damaged by disagreements. Finally, emotional intelligence helps us build resilience by managing and regulating our own emotions and coping with stress, allowing us to bounce back more quickly from setbacks. We can maintain and enhance our relationships by cultivating emotional intelligence, leading to a more fulfilling life.

Enhancing Emotional Intelligence:

Emotional intelligence is of great significance, and several strategies can help us enhance it. One such strategy is self-reflection. By taking some time regularly to reflect on our emotions and reactions, we can increase our self-awareness and identify areas that require improvement. Another effective strategy is mindfulness. Regularly practising mindfulness techniques like meditation can help us cultivate a present-centred awareness of our emotions, improving our ability to manage them. Empathy practice is yet another crucial component of emotional intelligence. It involves actively trying to understand and share the feelings of others, which can deepen our capacity for empathy. Lastly, learning and practising effective communication techniques can go a long way in improving our ability to express our emotions and understand those of others.

The connections we form throughout our lives significantly influence our emotional development and well-being. Emotional intelligence, rooted in the earliest relationships, is a critical skill set for navigating these connections, enhancing our ability to engage with others meaningfully and compassionately. We improve our lives and contribute to our communities' well-being by fostering emotional intelligence and creating a more empathetic and understanding world.

Regarding our relationships, it can be helpful to envision a landscape with concentric circles expanding outward. At the centre are our closest connections - our families - followed by our broader social circle, community, society, nation, and humanity. Our behaviour in these relationships is rooted in the values we hold and the decisions we make based on those values.

11

Modern Masculinity

Previously, I offered a different set of values for a New Vision of Masculinity. This new masculinity starts with being **inclusive** as opposed to the exclusivity that is integral to territoriality. **Democratic** rather than hierarchical, **distributive** instead of acquisitional and **cooperative** instead of competitive. So, how do we exercise the values of the New Masculinity in my relationships? Let's start with our life partner.

Being Inclusive

Earlier in the book, I spoke about a couple I had seen professionally who had become aware that they no longer felt connected. Their problem of having stopped including each other in their lives is reflective of a culture that has emerged over the last few decades. It is not completely new. As we have discussed, men and women have historically been relegated to separate spheres of life. This is perhaps just a different permutation of this separateness. However, it has some very negative consequences for our intimate relationships with our partners.

Some years ago, my wife and I began making some interesting observations. We'd be sitting in a restaurant, looking around, we would see a table of women sitting together having a good time. Then, when you went to a sporting venue, you would find groups of men together having a good time. Of course, we are all aware of the jokes about all the men around the barbie[2], and the women gathered in another part of the yard, but this was different. These were not outings where couples had arrived together and slipped into an informal gender-based division. These were separate social groups.

Over the years, it appears that this trend has continued to grow, and both of us became aware that many people we knew had regular social engagements that did not include their partners or family. Since both of us are therapists, we started to look at what was going on for the couples that we were seeing in counselling. An interesting pattern emerged that was consistent across many couples. Many couples conducted relationships that maintained a great deal of separateness between the two individuals. There was an emphasis on "me" time. The time that was spent in pursuit of their own interests, and often relationships with separate groups of friends. They would often holiday on their own or with 'the girls' or 'the guys'.

In the home, this separateness could result in strict divisions regarding how the chores and activities with the children were allocated to each parent. Most couples today are pushed for time to look after their individual careers and children. One of the consequences of the value placed on the world of

---

[2] A Grill

work is that everyone's sense of their own value resides in their participation in that world, and our economic reality has changed so that most families need two wages to cover their expenses. [This in itself is a very complex sociological and economic issue of patriarchy.]

However, within the context of couples' relationships, this 'time-poor' lifestyle has led to many having very little 'couples' time. Family time now has to be 'special', doing fun things together. These couples are no longer engaged in doing the ordinary day-to-day stuff together, including eating meals together. The opportunities to relate to each other as a couple and to the family as a group had diminished, and they all lived increasingly separate lives. It is no longer unusual in families for all of the members to be in separate areas of the house during the evening. In some wealthier families, even the care of the children is frequently outsourced to au pairs and nannies, meaning that apart from directing that care, there was no space in which, as a couple, they participated in the tasks of caring for children.

As with the couple I spoke about previously, these highly 'independent' relationships were all characterised by a very low state of energy. It was as if they had moved into a stagnant state. They also exhibited a low state of attachment. In most, I would argue that the individuals in the relationship are absent from one another, both physically and emotionally. They would know little about each other apart from the facts of their activities and movements, and even this was sometimes confined to notes on the calendar.

After time, this would translate into an ambivalence from both partners as to whether the relationship was 'worth' the struggles and challenges. Then, rather than looking inward at changing their relationship, they would look outside of the relationship to have their needs met. All of which would result in more of the same, and in some instances, even worse, one or both would embark on affairs with other people. These relationships had evolved into ones where each of the partners was excluding the other from large and important areas of their lives. Many divorces, with their pain and upheaval, have been the result of this form of insidious and unplanned detachment.

An inclusive approach to being a couple is one where the dyad of the couple is seen as the core around which we organise our lives. The very reason for being part of a couple is that the love and intimacy of this type of relationship provide us with a sense of well-being and emotional security that is vital for human flourishing. Together, if we have children, it gives us the support we need to nurture them and raise them so that they can thrive and have good, emotionally satisfying lives.

Intimacy is at the core of a strong relationship with our partners. If we are inclusive in how we approach each other, we can build on that intimacy, consolidating and enhancing it over time. By organising our lives so that couple time is valued and prioritised, we can lay the foundation to negotiate a more attached relationship that will be more satisfying and rewarding. And one that will engage our children in our family life, not only building those relationships but showing them how to create happy relationships for themselves in the future.

Being Democratic:

Democracy, in the way most of us use the idea, is about a system of government where power is vested in the people, who exercise power directly or through elected representatives. Key principles of democracy include political equality, majority rule, minority rights, and freedom of expression. In a democratic system, decisions are made based on the collective agreement of the majority while ensuring that the rights and voices of the minority are respected and protected.

But how does that apply to personal relationships? Applying the concept of democracy to interpersonal relationships offers a fascinating lens through which to view power dynamics, decision-making, and mutual respect in our relationships. In a democratic interpersonal relationship, similar principles would apply:

Equality: Each person in the relationship has an equal say and importance. This means decisions are not dominated by one individual but are made considering the perspectives and needs of both people.

Joint Decision-Making: Decisions are made through a process involving both parties' input and agreement. This mirrors the democratic principle of collective decision-making rather than autocratic or unilateral decision-making.

Freedom of Expression: Each individual in the relationship has the right to express their thoughts, feelings, and opinions freely and without fear of retribution or disregard.

Accountability and Responsibility: Each person is accountable for their actions and decisions within the relationship, akin to how elected representatives in a democracy are accountable to the electorate.

In the context of masculinity studies, this democratic approach to interpersonal relationships can be particularly insightful. Traditional narratives of masculinity often emphasise dominance, control, and unilateral decision-making, traits that are antithetical to democratic principles. By advocating for a democratic model in interpersonal relationships, we challenge these traditional narratives and promote a more egalitarian, respectful, and mutually empowering approach to masculinity.

This shift can have profound implications for how men engage in romantic, platonic, familial, or professional relationships, encouraging a move from traditional power hierarchies towards more balanced and equitable dynamics. Throughout history, the 'head of the household' concept has been prevalent and influential in shaping social norms and expectations. This idea has been ingrained in many of our lives through debates and discussions about its relevance in modern times. Recently, an older woman I am acquainted with, shared a conversation she had at her church group regarding this issue. The group was grappling with the question of who should be the head of the house, taking into account religious beliefs and gender equality. Despite their best efforts, they found it difficult to reconcile the two concepts. However, my friend, who has been a strong advocate for gender equality throughout her life, pointed out that there is no need for a 'head' of anything in a marriage between two consenting adults. Her insightful comment sparked a lively discussion and challenged the group to re-examine their assumptions and beliefs about traditional gender roles.

This naturally led to a lot of discussion about decision-making. Who would take the lead? What if the couple couldn't agree, she was asked. These questions and the difficulty the group had in thinking about a couple making decisions together, in consensus, is a direct result of patriarchy. Surely, in a marriage built on love and respect, the concept of being partners in your life together would naturally lead to a democratic approach to all decision-making that impacts the family.

Given our patriarchal upbringing, one of men's greatest challenges is to truly relate to women as equals. This means shedding parochial attitudes and subscribing to realities and not myths. Relating to someone as equal means not just paying lip service to their equality because of the law. It means truly seeing them in the same light as we see ourselves. A relationship of that kind means being more open with our thoughts and feelings and more responsive to our partner's thoughts and feelings. It means we need to learn to negotiate rather than dictate or manipulate to meet our needs. It also means being physically, emotionally, socially and spiritually available.

In a democratic relationship, we are both accountable for maintaining the respect and cooperation that is needed for it to remain stable. This means taking ownership of our part in its growth, and managing any conflict that arises, without shedding blame on the other or being contemptuous. How do we o that? By establishing and accepting that there is an inseparable relationship between my rights and my responsibilities and the other persons.

A relationship like that needs good tools. This will require good communication skills. And, more importantly, the willingness to stick to our values. In other words, I cannot just say that 'I love you', I have to show it. It can't be all about you or your partner. It has to be about both of you together, finding a way through the challenges of building a life that works for both of you and your shared goals.

Being Distributive:

The key word here is sharing. I'm not talking just about the material things in the relationship. What I am talking about is sharing from my heart and soul and being there for the good and the bad without complaint, and offering whatever support I can muster without thinking about what's in it for me.

So, what does being distributive in a relationship look like? When we talk about distributing our time and our emotional energy, we are talking about those areas of our relationships that are the most vulnerable to disharmony. For example, by prioritising your own individual interests over those of the relationship, the message you give is that the relationship is secondary. What you are looking for is balance. By being inclusive and democratic, you can negotiate your time and energy distribution.

Sometimes, the simplest thing to do is to generate Random Acts of Kindness. This is a phrase coined by Anne Herbert and published in 1993. Herbert promoted the idea that these acts towards the outside world would create a gentler, more empathic culture. Since one of the most important aspects of intimacy is empathy, acting in a way that increases that empathy will also increase the level of intimacy. By being kind, without any expectation of a reward, you are acting on your feelings of love and commitment to the other person.

This value certainly puts being greedy and selfish into the right context and leads us to the next area of alignment:

Being Cooperative:

Fostering trust in a relationship is crucial to fostering cooperation. Cooperation is the fundamental skill that sustains any relationship. It allows you to put all areas of alignment into practice within the context of your life partnership. Remember that being cooperative means working together and jointly towards a common goal.

A successful relationship is more than just caring for one another. It is about sharing a common direction and purpose as a couple. It is important to cooperate with your partner in order to meet each other's needs and to keep the relationship strong. Communication is key in any relationship, and respectfully expressing your thoughts and emotions is essential. Trust and honesty are also vital components of a healthy relationship, as they create a foundation of mutual respect and understanding. It is important to remember that every relationship is different, and what works for one couple may not work for another. However, by working together and putting in the effort, you can create a fulfilling and meaningful relationship that lasts a lifetime.

Most importantly, cooperation leads to trust. I often see couples where trust is at a low point. This is because somewhere in the relationship, an event breached cooperation. It could have been practical, like withholding time, attention or information. A good example is that in many relationships, men still control much of the resources and frequently make unilateral decisions without consulting their partner. In some cases, this is so severe as to end the relationship. Even worse, in some instances, it has ended up in court.

In addition to emotional issues that can lead to a breach of trust in a relationship, it's important to recognise the issue of coercive control. This can involve using intimidation, isolation, and manipulation tactics to maintain power and control over a partner. It's important to be aware of the signs of coercive control and to seek help if you or someone you know may be experiencing it.

So, what steps do we need to take to remedy this in a relationship?

Remember the formula for flow? This is where it comes into its own. The foundation of any relationship hinges on good communication skills, so an open and transparent conversation around our attachment is a good stepping-off point. It includes the ability to reinforce our attachment to each other non-judgmentally. In this way, we can progress by aligning our needs, desires and goals. The ability to do this leads to attunement.

Being Loving:

I think most of us make assumptions about what it means to be loving. Much of this is determined by our cultural and family background and dynamics. The reality of what we see, as opposed to what we are told, really comes into play here. It will have shaped our ideas about showing love and how we express it. The most important thing here is that love is not a noun. It is a verb wherein actions are the true benchmark. These can be located on our pyramid of well-being that I discussed in the early chapter of this book. We prioritise physical expressions, which include not only sexual intimacy but also affection, tenderness, and pleasing gestures. It's important to note that attending to physical expressions involves more than just sex.

For instance, when your partner is experiencing discomfort or distress, it's crucial to show empathy and concern. Taking the time to understand their wants and needs is also a vital aspect of this level.

Our level of comfort with showing affection often stems from our childhood experiences. I once spoke with a woman who revealed that her husband's family never hugged each other before she joined them. At first, they were taken aback by her displays of physical affection, but eventually came to appreciate her demonstration of love and learned to express it themselves. This story highlights the power of recognising the benefits of change. A simple gesture like a hug or a gentle squeeze of the hand can convey love instantly.

When it comes to being more attuned to your partner on a psychological level, there are a few examples of what that might look like. For instance, you might notice that your partner seems particularly stressed out after work, and you could offer to take on some of their responsibilities to help ease their load. Or, you might notice that your partner is feeling down and could use a pick-me-up, so you surprise them with their favourite meal or activity. By being empathic and observant of your partner's emotional needs, you can create a stronger connection and a more fulfilling relationship.

In any healthy relationship, it is essential to be able to appreciate and honour your partner's unique viewpoint, even if it differs from your own. This involves actively listening to their thoughts and ideas without immediately dismissing them based on preconceived notions or personal biases. Respectful communication and consideration of one another's opinions can lead to a deeper understanding and appreciation of each other's perspectives, ultimately strengthening the bond between partners. It is crucial to approach disagreements or differing viewpoints with an open mind and a willingness to learn and grow as a couple. By valuing and respecting each other's thoughts and ideas, partners can build a strong foundation of mutual trust and understanding.

Socially, loving means being there to support but not control or manipulate. For men, this means not hogging the limelight. Too often, I hear men disregarding the support and backup their partner has provided them in order for them to reach the success they have. However, even when we acknowledge that our success has been won with our partner's help, we must be careful not to locate that within the traditional view of women as adjuncts to men, 'the woman behind the man'. This trivialises the autonomy of women and the choices they make to provide their skills in what they would see as a joint project. It means recognising that her work, activities and interests are as important as yours, not secondary considerations. Remember, patriarchy makes us narcissistic.

Finally, what does loving mean on a spiritual level? Remember the earlier section. Spirituality means different things to different people. However, suppose we put it into the context of having a purpose that gives us meaning and hones our intentions for actions that include something other than ourselves. In that case, we can apply this in a meaningful way to our relationship with a partner.

By prioritising inclusivity, democracy, distribution, cooperation, and love in our shared lives, we can establish a deeply attuned and aligned relationship. This foundation benefits our partnership and creates a positive model for our children to follow in their relationships. Children often emulate their parents, even if they recognise their parents' relationship is less than ideal. Also, attempting to avoid repeating the same mistakes can sometimes lead to even more unsatisfying outcomes.

The Attachment Model and its Implications

The Attachment Model, as conceptualised by John Bowlby and later expanded by Mary Ainsworth, provides a framework for understanding how early relationships with caregivers shape an individual's emotional and relational patterns throughout life. This model is based on the premise that the nature of the attachment bond formed between an infant and their primary caregivers has profound implications for the individual's emotional regulation, exploration behaviour, and subsequent relationships.

Types of Attachment Styles

Bowlby and Ainsworth identified several attachment styles that describe the patterns of behaviour children exhibit towards their caregivers, which can then extend into their adult relationships:

1. Secure Attachment: Characterised by a healthy balance of attachment and autonomy. Securely attached individuals feel comfortable with intimacy and independence, trusting others and feeling confident in their relationships.

2. Anxious-Preoccupied Attachment: Marked by a high level of anxiety about relationships and a fear of abandonment. Individuals with this style tend to be overly dependent on others for validation and support.

3. Dismissive-Avoidant Attachment: Characterised by a strong sense of independence and self-sufficiency, often at the expense of close relationships. These individuals may dismiss

the importance of relationships and avoid intimacy.

4. Fearful-Avoidant (Disorganised) Attachment: Involves a combination of anxious and avoidant tendencies, with individuals often experiencing mixed feelings about closeness and difficulty trusting others. They may want intimacy but find it hard to trust and depend on others fully.

Implications of the Attachment Model and Emotional Regulation:

Attachment styles significantly influence how individuals manage and express their emotions. For example, securely attached individuals are generally better at regulating their emotions and seeking support in a balanced way, whereas those with insecure attachment styles may struggle with emotional regulation.

Relationship Patterns: The attachment style developed in early childhood often sets the template for adult romantic relationships. Secure attachment is associated with healthier, more satisfying relationships, while insecure attachment can lead to difficulties in forming and maintaining close relationships.

Resilience and Well-being: Secure attachment is linked to greater resilience in the face of stress and adversity. It also correlates with higher levels of well-being, as securely attached individuals are better equipped to seek out and receive social support.

Therapeutic Implications: Understanding an individual's attachment style can be invaluable in psychotherapy. It can provide insights into their relational dynamics and emotional challenges. Therapy can then aim to address and modify maladaptive attachment patterns, fostering a move towards secure attachment.

Imagine three individuals, A, B, and C.

A has a secure attachment style, feeling comfortable with both intimacy and autonomy. In relationships, A communicates needs and emotions effectively, seeks support when needed, and offers support to others.

B, with an anxious-preoccupied attachment style, fears abandonment and may cling to partners, seeking constant reassurance and struggling with self-worth.

C, exhibiting a dismissive-avoidant attachment style, values independence to the point of pushing others away, struggling to open up, and often appearing emotionally distant.

These simplified examples illustrate how early attachment experiences shape our approach to relationships, emotional expression, and coping mechanisms, highlighting the profound impact of attachment, which is about connection, across the lifespan. It is our attachment to others and our connection to our families, friends, colleagues and communities that have enabled humans to thrive. The importance of good secure attachment and connection for the well-being of us as individuals and for society as a whole can not be overstated.

12

Being a Great Dad

"My father gave me the greatest gift anyone could give another person; he believed in me." – Jim Valvano.

Breaking the Patriarchal Cycle:

In the complex tapestry of parenting, the nuanced role of fathers in the upbringing of both sons and daughters is a crucial element in developing young minds. As society progresses towards a deeper understanding of the social construction of gender dynamics and emotional intelligence, the traditional view of fatherhood is being reevaluated and expanded. This shift goes beyond the traditional enforcement of rules and discipline, focusing instead on imparting core values, fostering emotional regulation, ensuring consistent engagement, and nurturing secure attachment relationships. This approach to fathering, when infused with these principles, offers a transformative and holistic strategy for raising emotionally resilient, empathetic, and well-adjusted children. For sons, the father's role is instrumental in defining a healthy concept of masculinity that embraces emotional expression, empathy, and respect for all individuals, irrespective of sex, race, culture or other differences. Fathers set a critical example in demonstrating how to navigate emotions, manage relationships, and engage with the wider world. A father's influence is equally significant for daughters, impacting their self-esteem and emotional health and shaping their perspectives on relationships and social roles. The father-daughter dynamic is central to how young women perceive themselves and their place in the world.

This introduction leads us into a detailed exploration of value-based parenting practised by fathers, emphasising the crucial role of emotional regulation, the importance of consistency in parenting approaches, and the dedication required to build and sustain strong, nurturing attachment relationships. By delving into these key aspects, we aim to offer a comprehensive understanding of the transformative impact fathers can have in the lives of both their sons and daughters, preparing them to navigate life's challenges with confidence, empathy, and resilience.

In exploring masculinity and its transmission across generations, Dr. Michael Flood's recent study provides an incisive look into how fathers influence both their sons' understanding and expression of masculinity. This study, involving a significant sample of 839 pairs of young men and their fathers, delves into the heart of masculinity as a social construct, examining how attitudes and behaviours traditionally associated with masculinity are perpetuated within familial structures. Utilising a comprehensive dataset from a large-scale Australian health survey, Flood and his colleagues probe into various dimensions of masculinity, such as emotional expression, self-reliance, risk-taking, attitudes towards violence, the importance of appearing heterosexual, and the pursuit of dominance.

The findings of this research are pivotal in understanding the perpetuation of traditional masculinity norms. They highlight the critical role fathers play in modelling masculinity to their sons, raising profound questions about how masculinity is socially constructed and transmitted. The findings indicated a clear correlation between fathers' and sons' adherence to traditional masculinity. Young men who scored high on traditional masculinity measures usually had fathers with similar scores, particularly in areas like endorsing violence, the importance of appearing heterosexual, and the desirability of multiple sexual partners. This study underscores the role of social learning in shaping young people's attitudes and behaviours, highlighting the influence of fathers in passing on beliefs about masculinity. Consequently, it suggests that interventions promoting healthy masculinity among young people should also engage fathers, aiming to break this cycle of patriarchal transmission.

Building on these insights, , "Being a Great Dad," shifts focus to the practical implications of this research. It aims to provide a roadmap for fathers who wish to foster a more inclusive, empathetic, and balanced model of masculinity in their sons. This chapter will offer strategies for fathers to engage in positive, transformative masculinity, breaking the cycle of traditional norms and paving the way for healthier, more egalitarian models of manhood. In doing so, it underscores the potential for positive change in father-son dynamics, emphasising the power of intentional, mindful parenting in shaping the next generation of men.

The Issue for Dad:

Being a great father is a noble goal, but it's not always easy to achieve. Many men struggle to balance their own needs and desires with their children's, and it can be difficult to know where to start. One important thing to remember is that children learn by example, so it's essential to model the behaviours you want to see in your kids.

For example, if you want your children to be kind and compassionate, ensure you demonstrate those qualities in your interactions with them and others. If you want them to be resilient and persistent, show them how to bounce back from setbacks and keep pushing forward. On the other hand, if you had a difficult childhood and want to do things differently for your own kids, it's important to be intentional about the changes you want to make. Take time to reflect on what worked well for you growing up and what didn't, and consider how you can adjust your parenting style accordingly.

Ultimately, being a great father is about being present, attentive, and willing to learn and grow alongside your children. It's not always easy, but with patience, dedication, and a willingness to adapt, it's a goal that is well within reach.

Within the construct of patriarchy, the figure of the 'father' is commonly associated with power and authority. This is reflected in the hierarchies of our institutions, religious beliefs, and the traditional family dynamic, where the father is typically viewed as the head of the household, responsible for making decisions and administering justice. In the past, many children were warned of potential punishment from their fathers upon their return from work due to the child's misbehaviour. However, in recent decades, the notion of the authoritarian father has been challenged, and many men have deliberately chosen not to adhere to this stereotype. They do not wish to exert their power and authority in the same way as their own father figures.

It is important to recognise that women have rightfully rejected being powerless witnesses to their husbands' authority within the family. The traditional hierarchy of the home has caused significant harm, and as a result, many of us have shifted our approach to parenting. In the past, discipline and control were often associated with male power, and unfortunately, this sometimes led to abuse within families. However, the abundance of conflicting ideas in books and articles can be overwhelming and confusing when looking for new perspectives on parenting. Without clear guidance, many of us may feel disengaged or sidelined by our partners in the day-to-day parenting tasks.

An example of this is what caught my attention not long ago while I was standing outside a shop. It was that ear-shattering noise that only a pre-schooler can make when their parent, in this case, Dad, isn't satisfying their immediate demands. In blissful ignorance, Dad had broken some rule that, unbeknownst to him, he was not allowed to sit down in his son's presence. The boy was now giving full vent to his displeasure, both vocally and physically. Desperate to stay disinterested in the tantrum, Dad tried to ignore his offspring's terror tactics. Even a well-placed right hook from the boy failed to elicit any change in Dad's strategy.

I confess I was mesmerised. I watched as Dad's stoicism gave way to pleading glances thrown out into the universe. The subtext was crystal clear: Please! Rescue me, for I don't know what to do. But no intervention, divine or otherwise, arrived, and Dad had been abandoned and left to deal with this on his own. Whatever rescue he had hoped for was not going to happen, so Dad braced himself. Re-engaging with renewed optimism, he now pulled out the final weapon from his meagre arsenal: reason.

In spite of Dad's stoic attempt, reinforced by cool reason, his son remained steadfast in his assault, immune to logic and rational argument. Again, Dad desperately looked around, and suddenly, there was a change in his manner. A sense of relief flickered across his face. I tracked his gaze. A woman, looking harangued by her son's unruly behaviour, was approaching.

There was, however, no look of understanding or compassion for our paternal hero. On the contrary, I had difficulty deciding who she was more cross with, her son or husband. However, the truly telling thing was that Dad was now withdrawn completely. He didn't get up and walk away; he withdrew emotionally. Mum was left to placate the boy who, no doubt, will strike again. And, as he gets older, his behaviour will get uglier.

Now, there is a host of messages and lessons in this small tale of woe, but I want to start with this: we, as men, are in deep trouble when we absent ourselves from being a parent. When we can get emotionally KO'd by a four-year-old, what are our chances of coping with a fourteen-year-old? This is bad enough when your child is a boy, but many men feel even more helpless with their daughters, and this is a major problem because girls need their fathers as much as boys do.

In this situation, Dad appeared to have no authority or personal power. Well, you might say that Dad is just the poor schmuck who caught in my critical eye. But that's not the case.

In my practice, I spend a lot of time talking with men about issues just like the one I have described. Most acknowledge that their 'failures' have led to their wife or partner taking over. Even more problematic is when they allow themselves to be sidelined from the start. By not being part of the parenting process from the start when the children are small, a father has no history of ongoing parental authority on which to base any future parenting interactions. Both parents are important in all stages of childhood. It is important to remember that it is a feature of patriarchy to delineate parenting responsibilities by gender and according to children's ages. It is also vitally important to recognise that parenting is built on attachment and connection and like all relationships, it takes time.

When a father's parental relationship with his children has been diminished by his absence, whether that is physical or emotional, he finds himself at a loss about how to effectively deal with those critical times in a child's life when they need him to step up, to be authoritative and directive. The question is not whether fathers should be involved. The question is how a father should act as a parent to get the best response from their children. To give his children the direction they need.

How do we deal with a teenager who's challenging us? Do we get physical? Do we reason with him/her? What do we do? Many men, struggling to find the right answer to these questions, are working in the dark. Comments I get from many fathers include, 'I just felt like smacking him!' Or, 'if I could, I'd just throw him out of the house.' So, is the solution to use force or rejection?

It doesn't need to be either, but many men don't know the right way to approach their children. They are conflicted about what they feel and think is their role as a father. By the time their children are teenagers, they represent a considerable challenge, even to the dads who've had a strong and secure attachment to their children and who have been able to be present and available. It can become a harrowing time. Often the issues that must be dealt with involve safety issues around freedom of movement, risky behaviour and schooling, and a father's natural fear for their child can cripple them if they don't have a clear idea of their role within the relationship.

The question I pose to most fathers is, 'Where do you think you are in your relationship with your child?' I typically get one of three replies: I think I'm not there; I'm there, but I'm not sure I want to be, or he makes it so hard; and I hate to admit it, but I'm scared of him. Many of us Dads are either absent, ambivalent or anxious about our relationship with our children. Just as we are in our relationships with our partners, funny that, isn't it?

'What happened to that idyllic picture of my kid and me playing together, watching the footy[3] or going for a surf, sitting together on the lounge watching a movie? It wasn't meant to be this hard.'

The Issues for Sons:

By the time most of our sons are young adults, many have become distant and preoccupied with the tasks of their age group. The pressure to find their way in the world and the memories of conflicts, poorly handled, mixed with shame and blame, can discourage open communication with adults and their peers. Many fathers complain to me that they see very little of their son, let alone feel that they have a relationship

---

[3]

with him. The lyrics of Cat's in the Cradle by Harry Chapin come to mind:

'He came to the world in the usual way

But there were planes to catch and bills to pay

He learned to walk while I was away, And he was talking 'fore I knew it, and as he grew,

He'd say, "I'm gonna be like you, Dad, You know I'm gonna be like you."

A father's unconscious negative behaviours, actions and attitudes can continue to have an impact in so many ways throughout our own and our children's lives. But is this the legacy we want for our sons? Surely we want more for ourselves and our sons?

The transition from boyhood to adulthood is fraught with challenges, not least of which is the evolving relationship between sons and their fathers. This complex dynamic is influenced by a myriad of factors, from social expectations to personal experiences of conflict and misunderstanding. The lyrics of Harry Chapin's song poignantly encapsulate this estrangement, vividly depicting the missed opportunities and the cyclical nature of paternal absence and the subsequent loss of connection.

Psychological Perspectives

Attachment Theory posits that early interactions with caregivers form the blueprint for future relationships. When fathers are physically or emotionally absent, sons may struggle to form secure attachments, leading to difficulties in trust and communication in later life.

Social Learning Theory suggests that sons learn to be men

primarily by observing their fathers. Negative behaviours, attitudes, and unresolved conflicts are often unconsciously mimicked, perpetuating a legacy of detachment and dissatisfaction.

Erikson's Stages of Psychosocial Development highlight the adolescent crisis of identity vs. role confusion, where sons seek to establish their individuality. Conflicts with fathers during this stage can exacerbate feelings of alienation and hinder the development of a healthy sense of self.

Historical and Social Influences

Throughout history, social norms have dictated rigid roles for men, emphasising stoicism, dominance, and emotional restraint. These expectations can stifle open communication between fathers and sons, leaving little room for vulnerability or empathy.

The industrial and digital revolutions have transformed the traditional household, often increasing the physical and emotional distance between fathers and sons. The demands of modern work life mean that many fathers find themselves absent during pivotal moments of their sons' development, echoing the narrative of Cat's in the Cradle.

The Impact of Contemporary Culture

The modern crisis of masculinity, fuelled by changing gender roles and expectations, has left many men questioning their identity and worth. This existential uncertainty can be particularly destabilising for the father-son relationship, as both struggle to reconcile their personal experiences with the evolving social conception of what it means to be a man.

To break the cycle of distance and disconnection, it is essential to foster open lines of communication, encourage emotional expression, and redefine masculinity in a way that embraces vulnerability and mutual respect. Engaging in shared activities and actively working to understand each other's perspectives can help bridge the gap between fathers and sons, building a foundation for a stronger, more fulfilling relationship.

The legacy we leave for our sons should not be one of distance and misunderstanding but of connection, understanding, and growth. By challenging outdated norms, addressing unresolved conflicts, and fostering open communication, fathers and sons can work together to build a new legacy of mutual respect and understanding, moving beyond the shadows of the past into a brighter, more connected future.

But What About Fathers and Daughters?

Here's a News Flash! Fathering a daughter is different to fathering a boy. As a therapist, coach, mentor, and father to a daughter, I can confidently say that fathering a girl is a unique experience that presents various challenges. All children are exposed to social pressures that dictate how they should look and behave to be deemed "popular." Unfortunately, for girls, this often means they are discouraged from being too intelligent, as smart girls may appear threatening to boys. This is now occurring at a younger age than in the past due to social media.

Additionally, stereotypes surrounding clothing, sports, and sex, all of which become an issue much earlier than most parents expect them to, can exacerbate these issues. Fathers of teenage girls also face the challenge of guiding their daughters through the complexities of dating and navigating that dangerous digital world. All of these challenges can make fatherhood a difficult path to navigate. While some fathers may retreat from these issues, it's important to remember that conflicts will inevitably arise, and it's crucial to address them head-on. This is why it is vital that you and your daughter's other parent work together. By aligning yourselves according to your shared values and love for your children, you can minimise the problems caused by conflicting messages and expectations.

Irrespective of whether you are parenting a son or a daughter, being present, engaged and consistent as a parent will not only give them the support and love they need to grow into happy adults, but it will also give you the rewards of a loving relationship with them.

Fathering a daughter is a special mission because you are their example of manhood. The expectations you have of your daughter and the way you relate to her will not only develop your own relationship with her but also demonstrate to her what the world thinks of her as a girl and soon-to-be woman. As she grows and is exposed to various ideas of girlhood, her home environment and her parents should have the most influence. As we have discussed before, it will be what she sees you do and what she experiences in her relationship with you that will matter.

Many fathers withdraw as their daughters move into adolescence. Yet, this is just the time when girls need their Dads! This is the time when they need as good a model of a man as we can give them. Within the father-daughter relationship, your daughter will develop her sense of self in the context of relationships with boys and men. Her belief in her right to respect and to be valued as an autonomous human being able to make her own decisions is determined by her experience of her relationship with her father and what she witnessed in the relationship between her parents.

Being a parent is about teaching your child how to live in the world with others, how to be comfortable in their skin, value their strengths while being aware of their flaws, and engage in high-quality relationships that are inclusive, democratic, distributive, and cooperative.

Dr Mark Regnerus, a sociologist at the University of Texas at Austin, conducted a study highlighting the influence of father-daughter relationships on the timing of daughters' first sexual experiences. The study, published in the "Journal of Family Issues" [2006], analysed data from about 10,000 seventh through 12th-grade students living in two-parent households, sourced from the National Longitudinal Study of Adolescent Health. This study offers illuminating insights into the dynamics of parent-child relationships and their impact on adolescents' sexual behaviour. Although the research identifies additional factors that appear to delay the onset of sexual activity among girls, including religious service attendance and the educational level of their mothers, it is their relationship with their fathers that is of critical importance.

This research highlights the profound influence of the father-daughter relationship on the timing of daughters' initial sexual activities. The study reveals that girls who enjoy very high-quality relationships with their fathers are significantly less likely to engage in early sexual activity compared to those who report poor-quality relationships. In fact, girls with low-quality father-daughter relationships are nearly twice as likely to initiate sexual activity at an earlier age compared to their counterparts who have strong, positive relationships with their fathers.

Interestingly, the study did not find a similar correlation when examining the relationships girls have with their mothers or the relationship between boys and either of their parents. This specificity suggests a unique aspect of the father-daughter bond in influencing daughters' decisions regarding sexual activity. These findings emphasise the critical role fathers play in their daughters' lives, especially concerning their sexual development and decision-making processes. The study enriches our understanding of father-daughter relationships through its detailed analysis, shedding light on their significant social and developmental consequences.

13

Men Within Society

Making Good Men Great is about helping men to go from simply surviving to thriving. It is time to beat a different drum. The time has come to fundamentally address the issues that are killing boys and men in unprecedented numbers. We need to include a framework in our conversations that allows a constructive perspective on the evolution of masculinity.

But how do we do this? My wife and I looked closely at the possible connotations of using the word leadership in this section, a word or idea that she thought could be mistaken for perpetuating patriarchy. I appreciate where she is coming from. But I am already exercising leadership in questioning patriarchy and looking to do something about it, just like the many women in history who have stepped out of the confines of the restrictions placed upon them by this male ideology, who showed leadership. Many women and men have stepped up to address the social constraints of bigotry, racism, misogyny, and other authoritarian ideologies and, to do so, have become leaders.

In my view, leadership is first and foremost about service. It is about being influential. This does not mean being manipulative, a devious and dishonest use of position and information often used by both the powerful and the powerless to get what they want. It means that a true leader, someone with influence irrespective of sex, race, religion, or ethnicity, must be open, collaborative, and authentic.

The values we have been considering previously, inclusive, distributive, democratic, and cooperative, will help us move beyond patriarchy. But before we can move into this new paradigm of masculinity, we need to ask some really tough questions about what we really want masculinity to look like.

What is it that we want from men in our society?

What do men want from other men?

What do women want from men?

What are the real roles of men in the here and now of the 21st century?

If we reimagine masculinity, can we reimagine society?

And for what reasons?

And who is going to do it?

This list of questions could go on for several more paragraphs, and I'd still not exhaust it. Nor do I think that we are asking the right questions. In fact, I'm in search of more meaningful, better questions in this regard. But in the meantime, these are a good start.

In the main, I believe I have made a good argument that patriarchy, the ideology of the Iron Age Warrior, needs to be abandoned, and in its place, something better needs to take shape, something that serves men, women and society better.

I have also argued that men as individuals need to get to know themselves through reflection and use their insights into their own way of being in their own lives to make changes that will enhance their relationships and emotional wellbeing. But as a group, we also need to reflect on the bigger picture of men and reimagine and rethink how we men can be. This will require that we have at least some idea about the history of masculinity, how it has shaped gender culture, how this has influenced our ideas of relationships, economics, and politics and, most importantly, how this has impacted men psychologically and emotionally.

Now, the mere fact that you have gotten this far into the book means that you are thinking about these issues and wondering what you, and any of us, can do about the state of men and masculinity. You have reached beyond the horizon. You have, in essence, a curiosity, if not a thirst, for something different and are reaching into the deeper parts of yourself. Perhaps this curiosity is strong enough to think clearly about what you can contribute. If this is the case, you're already part of the movement. Because you are engaging in forging a new vision of what masculinity can mean. And this is not simply about being more emotionally expressive. We need to embrace being whole, physically, psychologically and socially. How can we focus on a pathway that will help us evolve as individuals and as a group?

Those of you who are actively involved in a sport will probably have, at some point, engaged a coach to help you 'improve your game.' Most of these coaches and mentors are generally task-specific, at least in sports. They help you to focus on specific areas of action. Academics and professionals will also seek out mentors and coaches to help foster their careers, and maybe you have either done this, or thought about doing this; however, what we need is a mentoring process in a broader sense.

In this context, working through a curriculum that allows you to develop yourself physically, psychologically, professionally and socially is more useful. A curriculum that challenges old, archaic assumptions about being a man and assumptions about what women are about, and replaces it with something that makes you more flexible and, therefore, resilient.

Are you part of a curriculum that makes you a good all-rounder? For most men, professional or not, the answer is no. Firstly, because there has not really been one. There have been many observations about what we, men, are deficient in and how to rectify that. However what we need is to reflect on masculinity from a positive, constructive and global perspective in order to understand how to create a framework for our evolution beyond patriarchy. A process of going from good to great.

As men, we have faced significant challenges with the changing world that has challenged our privileged position. The response to this has been a resurgence of patriarchy. However, we need to have a clear vision and avoid regressing to the Iron Age. We need to be courageous and step out of the toxic confines of patriarchy to create a new masculinity that supports and sustains our communities and diverse cultures. But we cannot achieve this alone. We must form close, intimate relationships that create support and reflection and encourage networks. It is time for us to embrace courage and work together towards creating a better future.

We're in a pivotal era, ripe with the potential to draft a comprehensive blueprint for men to excel in every facet of their lives. This design encompasses fostering robust relationships, contributing to societal betterment, personal development, financial wellness, and civic engagement, all aiming to empower men to reach their highest potential authentically and make a positive imprint on the world.

For men to succeed in leadership and life, it's crucial to invest in personal growth. Such success hinges on a clear vision, the cultivation of meaningful connections, and the ability to communicate in a manner that inspires others. These endeavours should be underpinned by values that not only serve personal interests but also advance the collective good. These principles compel us to chase after worthy objectives and motivate others to align with our mission. Historical figures like Mandela and Gandhi leveraged their vision and oratorical prowess to galvanise nations, showcasing how shared values and compelling communication can catalyse change. Similarly, embracing sustainable practices can initiate a shift in communal behaviours towards more environmental stewardship. This narrative underscores the significance of having a well-defined vision, robust values, and effective communication skills as foundational elements to enact considerable influence and cultivate a culture of excellence and communal advancement.

Cultures are dynamic entities, capable of evolving in response to internal and external pressures. Over the past two centuries, a seminal cultural shift in the Western world has been the evolution of women's roles in society. Pioneers like Mary Wollstonecraft and Harriet Taylor mounted challenges against entrenched views on women's rights, sparking a discourse that precipitated significant cultural transformations.

Thanks to collective action and steadfast determination, women have made substantial strides in education, employment, and political representation. However, these advancements have come at a considerable cost, with many women facing sacrifices and adversities. Despite notable progress, pressing issues like gender-based violence, wage disparity, and discrimination persist, underscoring the ongoing struggle for equality.

The metamorphosis of women's societal roles underscores the potency of collective action and persistence in the face of challenges. It highlights the necessity of questioning established norms and collaborating to engender positive societal change. This journey exemplifies the capacity for cultural evolution and underscores the continued imperative for advocacy for equality.

The European Industrial Revolution marked a significant cultural shift, transitioning human occupations from primarily agricultural to manufacturing bases, illustrating how cultures adapt to new realities. A similar evolution is observable in Asia today, signifying that cultures, whether at the societal, organisational, or institutional levels, morph to accommodate new circumstances. The challenge for visionaries lies in ensuring that these transformations benefit everyone, not just a select few, addressing a historical pattern of exclusivity in societal, institutional, and business changes.

As a visionary, it's crucial to acknowledge that optimal outcomes emerge when the social, organisational, team and individual cultures coalesce around core values and behaviours, implemented with integrity and sustainability. Therefore, each pillar should be viewed in relation to the others, with each contributing dynamically to the next, enhancing our collective and individual consciousness of our vision and values that are fundamental to ourselves and our society. We cannot merely scrutinise the individual man to identify flaws or engage solely in abstract ideological debates. We must appreciate the interplay among various levels within an ecological framework that prioritises interdependence while allowing for individual expression.

Imagine the profound transformations possible in our families, communities, workplaces, and society at large if we were to wholeheartedly embrace the principles of the New Masculinity—values of inclusivity, democracy, distributive justice, and cooperation. Let's envisage a world where these ideals lead our interactions, driving positive change and nurturing deep, meaningful connections.

Summary

Embarking on the transformative journey outlined in *Making Good Men Great: Surfing a New Masculinity* invites us to a profound exploration of self and society, where personal growth serves as the cornerstone for social transformation. This odyssey isn't just about individual renaissance; it's a blueprint for restructuring the social edifice itself, challenging us to re-conceptualise our identities within a framework that seeks equity and justice for all.

At the heart of this quest lies the recognition that patriarchy, with its deep-rooted tentacles, isn't merely a dilemma for half the world's population but a pervasive scourge that distorts human connections and social structures universally. Our liberation from these chains mandates a bold departure from patriarchal ideologies, a journey enriched by education that hones our critical faculties enhances our emotional intelligence and deepens our understanding of not only gender dynamics but social and political habits that no longer work for us. It's an education that doesn't just illuminate minds but transforms hearts, fostering a worldview where human equality becomes the norm, not the exception.

The dialogue for change is a clarion call to action, urging us to cultivate spaces where men can engage in open, honest conversations about personal transformation and social evolution. These dialogues are envisioned as sanctuaries of introspection, accountability, and growth, enabling men to dissect and dismantle the patriarchal norms ingrained within and around them. Through such reflective conversations, men can confront and overcome the biases and behaviours that perpetuate inequality, embracing a new paradigm of masculinity marked by empathy, respect, and equity.

To embody a non-patriarchal culture, we must commit to principles of inclusivity, democracy, fairness, and cooperation, championing these values across all spheres of life. This commitment involves not just promoting diversity and equality but also actively dismantling systems and structures that perpetuate all divisive categories and biases. It calls for a collective effort to redefine social norms and values, encouraging collaboration and mutual respect in place of competition and dominance.

I call on men, in particular, to lead this charge, to hold themselves and each other accountable for sexist, classist and intolerant actions and attitudes. This requires a courageous willingness to call out these behaviours, engage in self-reflection on personal biases, and take proactive steps towards change. Furthermore, this journey demands a radical transformation in the socialisation of boys, instilling in them from a young age the values of kindness, empathy, and equality, thereby disrupting the cycle of divisive patriarchal ideologies being passed down through generations.

Central to our mission is the critical examination and reform of our political, economic, and religious institutions to root out patriarchal underpinnings that have long influenced their direction and policies. This includes advocating for systemic changes that promote equality for all of the members of our community and ensuring that our educational systems become beacons of inclusivity, diversity, and fairness. Such reforms are essential not only for creating a more equitable society but also for building a world that truly reflects the rich diversity of human experience.

Picture this journey as mastering the art of surfing upon the waves of new masculinity. Like any noble pursuit, the initial challenge is formidable, yet it heralds the dawn of a journey filled with limitless potential and exhilarating adventures. As we navigate these waves, pushing the boundaries of conventional masculinity, we embark on a path of self-discovery and collective transformation. This voyage calls for bravery, an openness to confront our vulnerabilities, and an unwavering commitment to growth and learning.

It's crucial to remember that we do not walk this path alone. A vanguard of pioneers has paved the way, and a community of like-minded individuals walks with us. Together, we have the power to redefine masculinity and shape a world where men are celebrated for their compassion, integrity, and dedication to fostering positive change.

Therefore, let us take this step forward together, with a resolve to manifest the best within ourselves and to inspire the same in others. Let us forge a world where every man can flourish, contributing to a legacy that uplifts and transforms the very fabric of our society. In embracing this journey from good to great, we ride the waves of a new masculinity towards a future brimming with hope, unity, and profound transformation.

"The Odyssey of Being Human: A Tribute to the Noble Heart"

In the realm where noble hearts reside, a great man lives, guided by his purpose. He aligns his vision with blood, sweat, and tears, not with empty platitudes. His truth is authentic and pure.

His eyes see a world that is a canvas to be amended. He extends his love to himself and others. He envisions a better life with dreams so bold, bringing them to reality with his great heart.

The drum of courage beats within his chest. He faces each test, stepping up to life. In emotional battles where fears reside, he shows up with no truths hidden.

A beacon of strength, yet vulnerable and raw, his heart is wide open like a lion's roar. Humility adorns him, self-reflection his mirror. He holds himself dear in the eyes of a great man.

His life was a harmonious ode, a melody entwined with the very fabric of the universe, a dance with the elements and the celestial bodies, extending an olive branch to all of creation, embracing the cycle of existence from the golden dawn to the tranquil dusk.

Empathy is his language, understanding his speech. "The eyes of a great man reveal compassion that touches every heart.". He truly feels the joy and pain of others, healing their wounds with his empathy.

A fortress of confidence, yet not of conceit, he stands self-assured, meeting every challenge. He is soaked in his worth, needing no others' approval. His self-belief is evoked by truth.

In the realm where noble hearts reside, a great man lives, guided by his purpose. His legacy of actions and the tales they share live on. The spirit of a great man, his essence, is everywhere.

Glossary of Terms

Acquisitional

A core value of patriarchy is characterised by the pursuit and accumulation of resources, wealth, and material possessions, often at the expense of others or ethical considerations. It emphasises material success as a measure of self-worth and social status.

Affluenza

A condition characterised by feelings of envy, regret, and shame due to not meeting societal standards of ambition, acquisition, and financial affluence. It often leads to a constant sense of dissatisfaction and the need for more material wealth.

Androgyny

A concept suggesting the presence of both masculine and feminine traits in an individual. This term challenges traditional gender roles and stereotypes, promoting a more fluid and inclusive understanding of gender identity.

Authenticity

A multifaceted concept encompassing self-expression, emotional awareness, vulnerability, and integrity. It involves expressing oneself in alignment with one's values and beliefs, embracing vulnerability, and living independently from external validation.

Being Soulful

A stage in the evolution of masculinity that integrates knowledge with empathy, introspection, and a profound sense of purpose. It transforms knowledge into wisdom and aligns actions with a broader understanding of one's place in the world.

Biological Determinism

The belief is that biological factors such as genetics determine human behaviour and social roles. This idea is often used to justify traditional gender roles and inequalities by attributing them to natural, unchangeable differences between sexes.

Big History

An interdisciplinary approach that explores the history of the universe from the Big Bang to the present, integrating knowledge from cosmology, physics, chemistry, biology, anthropology, and history to provide a comprehensive narrative of existence.

Cognitive-behavioural Therapy (CBT)

A type of psychotherapeutic treatment that helps individuals understand the thoughts and feelings that influence behaviours. CBT is commonly used to treat a range of mental health issues, including anxiety and depression, by challenging and changing unhelpful cognitive distortions and behaviours.

Combativeness
The tendency to engage in confrontational and aggressive behaviours, often arising from social expectations that valorise dominance, strength, and assertiveness as markers of masculinity.

Competitive
A patriarchal value that emphasises rivalry and the pursuit of victory over others. It often leads to behaviours focused on winning at all costs, fostering an environment where cooperation and empathy are undervalued.

Connectedness
A sense of belonging and meaningful relationships with others. It involves emotional intimacy, empathy, and shared experiences that foster a sense of community and support.

Emotional Courage
The bravery to confront and express one's emotions honestly, even when they are uncomfortable or vulnerable. It signifies a deep understanding of one's emotional landscape and the strength to be authentic.

Emotional Security
Understanding and being comfortable with one's identity and character, fostering emotional courage and the ability to make decisions aligned with one's values. It provides a foundation for healthy relationships and personal well-being.

Existential Crisis
A moment of profound questioning about the meaning,

purpose, and value of one's life. It often involves reflection on one's identity, roles, and relationships, leading to a deeper understanding of oneself.

Gender-role Stress
The anxiety and discomfort experienced when individuals feel they are not living up to societal expectations of their gender roles. This stress can negatively impact mental health and overall well-being.

Hierarchical
A patriarchal value that organizes individuals into ranked levels of authority and status, often leading to power imbalances and social inequality. It reinforces a top-down structure where those at the top exert control over those below.

Holistic Approach
A method of treatment or understanding that considers the whole person, including physical, emotional, mental, and social factors, rather than just symptoms or specific issues. It aims to achieve overall well-being and balance.

Hyper-masculinity
An exaggerated form of masculinity associated with aggression, dominance, and a disregard for emotions and vulnerability. It often leads to high stress and anxiety levels and can negatively impact both men and women.

Inclusivity
Incorporating an "and/also" perspective instead of a divisive "either/or" approach, fostering equality and respect. It

encourages forming supportive and loving relationships and considering ideas from a broader perspective.

Iron Age Warrior

A metaphor for traditional masculinity characterised by traits such as physical strength, dominance, and competitiveness. It reflects an outdated model of manhood that struggles to adapt to modern societal changes.

Mindfulness

Focusing on the present moment with awareness and without judgment is a mental practice that is often used as a therapeutic technique to reduce stress and increase emotional regulation.

Narrative Therapy

A form of psychotherapy that uses storytelling to help individuals understand and reshape their personal narratives, leading to personal growth and healing.

Patriarchy

An entrenched system of beliefs and assumptions about human nature that dictates social norms based on gender. It often results in the subjugation of women and the reinforcement of rigid gender roles. Patriarchy privileges male dominance and devalues traits associated with femininity.

Psychodynamic Therapy

A therapeutic approach that explores how unconscious thoughts and feelings influence behaviours. It aims to increase self-awareness and understanding of past experiences that shape current behaviour.

Spiritual Engagement

A form of engagement that goes beyond traditional religious practices, it involves connecting with something greater than oneself through various means, such as nature, meditation, art, or community. It fosters a sense of purpose and interconnectedness.

Territorial

A patriarchal value that emphasises the control and ownership of space, resources, and people. It often leads to behaviours that are protective, possessive, and exclusionary.

Toxic Masculinity

Aspects of masculinity that reinforce harmful behaviours such as aggression, emotional stoicism, and dominance. It is linked to negative outcomes like mental health struggles and strained relationships.

Traditional Masculinity

A set of cultural norms and expectations that define manhood based on traits like physical strength, emotional stoicism, dominance, and competitiveness. It often excludes or devalues traits such as empathy and vulnerability.

Vulnerability

Openly expressing a range of emotions, including those often suppressed in traditional masculinity, such as sadness, fear, or hurt. It is considered a strength that signifies emotional maturity and self-awareness.

This combined glossary provides detailed definitions and explanations to enhance understanding of the key concepts discussed in *Making Good Men Great: Surfing a New Masculinity.*

References

Beck, J. S. (2011). "Cognitive behaviour therapy: Basics and beyond". Guilford Press.

Biddulph, S. (2018). "Raising Boys in the 21st Century: How to Help Our Boys Become Open Hearted, Kind and Strong Men". HarperCollins.

Connell, R. W. (1995). "Masculinities". Polity Press.

Crenshaw, K. (1991). "Mapping the Margins: Intersectionality, Identity Politics, and Violence against Women of Color". Stanford Law Review, 43(6), 1241–1299.

Davis, A. (1983). "Women, Race, and Class". Vintage Books.

de Beauvoir, S. (1949). "The Second Sex". Parsley, H. M., Trans. (1952) Knopf.

De Botton, A. (2005). "Status Anxiety". Vintage Books.

Doherty, W. J., & McHale, S. M. "The Psychology of Family Dynamics".

Du Bois, W. E. B. (1903). "The Souls of Black Folk".

Ellis, A., & Harper, R. A. (2016). "A Guide to Rational Living". Wilshire Book Company.

Fausto-Sterling, A. (2000). "Sexing the Body". New York Basic Books.

Foucault, M. (1978). "The History of Sexuality, Volume 1: An Introduction". Translated by Robert Hurley. New York: Pantheon Books.

Fugère, M. A. "The Social Psychology of Love and Attraction".

Gender and Education. (2013). In G. Waylen (Ed.), The Oxford Handbook of Gender and Politics (pp. 327-343). Oxford University Press.

Gray, J. "Men are From Mars, Women are from Venus". [1992] Harper Collins.

Goleman, D. (2005). "Emotional Intelligence: Why It Can Matter More Than IQ". Bantam Books.

Goleman, D. (1995). "Emotional intelligence: Why it can matter more than IQ. Hierarchies in Politics, Economics and Commerce". Bantam Books.

Harvey, D. (2005). "A Brief Histoy of Neoliberalism". Oxford Uni Press.

Holtzworth-Munroe, A., & Stuart, G. L. (1994). "Typologies of Male Batterers: Three Subtypes and the Differences Among Them". Psychological Bulletin, 116(3), 476.

hooks, b. (2000). "Feminism is for Everybody". Passionate politics. Pluto Press.

Jewkes, R, Flood, M, Lang, J, (2015). "The Lancet"; 385(9977)1580-1589.

Johnson, A. G. (2005). "The Gender Knot: Unraveling Our Patriarchal Legacy". Temple University Press.

Kasser, T. [2016] 'Materialistic Values and Goals', in "Annual Review of Psychotherapy 67",

pp 489-514.

Kimmel, M. (2008). "Guyland: The Perilous World Where Boys Become Men". Harper Collins.

Kimmel, M. S. (2017). "Healing from hate: How Young Men Get Into—and Out Of—Violent Extremism". University of California Press.

Kimmel, M. (2013). "Angry White Men: American Masculinity at the End of an Era". Nation Books.

Krznaric, R. (2014). "Empathy: Why it Matters and How to Get It". Penguin/Random House.

Leahy, R. L. (2017). "Cognitive Therapy Techniques: A Practitioner's Guide". Guilford Press.

Lorde, A. (1984). "Sister Outsider: Essays and speeches".

Mackay, H. (2014). "The Art of Belonging". Pan Macmillan. Australia

Marmot, M. (2005). 'Social determinants of health inequalities'. "The Lancet", 365(9464), 1099-1104.

Maslow, A,H. (1943). 'A Theory of Human Motivation'. in "Psychological Review", 50(4)

pp 370-396.

Marx, K., & Engels, F. (1848). The communist manifesto..

Mental Health Foundation (2020). Mental Health statistics retrieved from

https://www.mentalhealth.org.uk/statistics/mental-health-statistics-mental-health-foundation

Messner, M. A. (2016). "Some Men: Feminist Allies and the Movement to End Violence Against Women". Oxford University Press.

O'Donnell, O, 'Income Equality and Mental Health: A Causal Review.' [2018] "Social Science and Medicine", 198, pp 226-236.

Pateman, C. (1988). "The Sexual Contract". Stanford University Press.

Perales,F., Kuskoff, E., Flood, M., & King, T. (2023). "Like Father, Like Son: Empirical Insights Into the Intergenerational Continuity of Masculinity Ideology and Sex Roles". 88(9-10), 399-412.

Peterson, J. B. (2018). "12 Rules for Life: An Antidote to

Chaos". Random House Canada.

Pratto, F., Sidanius, J., Stallworth, L. M., & Malle, B. F. (1994). 'Social Dominance Orientation: A Personality Variable Predicting Social and Political Attitudes'. "Journal of Personality and Social Psychology", 67(4), 741.

Regnerus, M., & Luchies, L. B. (2006). 'The Parent-Child Relationship and Opportunities for Adolescents' First Sex'. "Journal of Family Issues", 27(2), 159-183.

Rogers, C.R. (1961) "On Becoming a Person: A Therapist's View of Psychotherapy". Constable (London)

Ronningstam, E. (2016). 'Narcissistic personality disorder: A clinical perspective'. "Journal of Psychiatric Practice", 22(6), 457-467. doi: 10.1097/PRA.0000000000000191

Rousseau, J-J. (1762), "Emile, or On Education". (Bloom, A., Trans 1979). Basic Books.

Sen, A. (1990). In I. Tinker (Ed.), "Persistent Inequalities" (pp. 43-59). New York: Oxford University Press.

Sidanius, J., & Pratto, F. (1999). "Social Dominance: An Intergroup Theory of Social Hierarchy and Oppression". Cambridge University Press.

Smith, Smith, Dorothy E. (1987). The everyday world as problematic: A feminist sociology. Boston: Northeastern University Press. ISBNs are 155553015X and 1555530370 . E. (1987).

Sternberg, R. J. "The New Psychology of Love".

Stiglitz, J. E. (2012). "The Price of Inequality: How Today's Divided Society Endangers our Future". WW Norton and Co.

Tomson, S. (2013). "The Code: The Power of 'I Will'". Patagonia.

Wilkinson, R., & Pickett, K. (2010). "The Spirit Level: Why More Equal Societies Almost Always Do Better". Penguin UK.

Williams, M. (2023), *The Connected Species*. Rowman and Littlefield.

Women and Education. (2001). In J. Worell (Ed.), "Encyclopaedia of Women and Gender,

vol. 2", (pp. 1431-1438). Academic Press.

Women and Higher Education. National Women's History Museum. Retrieved from https://www.womenshistory.org/articles/women-and-higher-education.

About the Author

Gunter Swoboda

Meet Gunter Swoboda, a renowned psychologist, speaker, author, and producer based in Australia. He is a member of the Australian Psychological Society and practices in Mona Vale, New South Wales. Gunter has more than 40 years of experience in counselling, coaching, and consulting. He specialises in helping men, couples, and families with various issues such as stress, anxiety, depression, anger, addiction, trauma, and relationship problems. He adopts a holistic and integrative approach in his practice that includes psychodynamic, cognitive-behavioural therapy (CBT), mindfulness, positive psychology, and narrative therapy.

In addition to his professional practice, Gunter is a prolific writer and speaker. He has authored several books, including *Making Good Men Great: Surfing a New Masculinity*. He has also delivered a TEDx talk on "How to Make Good Men Great." In addition, Gunter is a creative producer who has developed podcasts, documentaries, and web series that explore the themes of masculinity, leadership, and social change.

Gunter's ultimate goal is to inspire men to embrace their full potential and positively impact the world. He strongly believes that by redefining the narrative of masculinity, men can become more compassionate, courageous, and connected.

Lorin Josephson

Lorin Josephson holds a Bachelor of Arts (Honours) and a Master of Arts in Organisational Ethics and has had an extensive career as a mental health clinician. Lorin believes that philosophy can provide practical wisdom for life's difficult questions and help us act authentically in the world. Having studied philosophy, history, and psychotherapy extensively, she has used the knowledge she has gained in both her personal and professional life. Her academic work focuses on individuals and their relationships, exploring how we become who we are and how our experiences shape the way we critically reflect on our values and the ethics that guide our lives.

Additionally, she has worked as an ethicist in her own practice.

You can connect with me on:
- https://www.gunterswoboda.com
- https://x.com/gunterswoboda
- https://facebook.com/GoodMenGreat
- https://www.philosophiesforliving.net
- https://www.goodmengreat.com

Subscribe to my newsletter:

✉ https://www.bonfirecinema.com/bonfirevip

www.ingramcontent.com/pod-product-compliance
Lightning Source LLC
Chambersburg PA
CBHW031147020426
42333CB00013B/556